Legend and Lore of Clayton, California.

E. Byrd

ISBN-13:

978-1523899630

ISBN-10:

1523899638

Published by: Gussethunters Printing (2016)

Edited by: Lisa Jahnke and Jenny Hosel.

Dedicated to Baby Corlis and Grandson Aiden

A huge thank you must go out to: The Clayton Historical Society; the Clayton Club Saloon, The City of Clayton; Richard Taylor and other local residents that have helped produce this book; Lisa Jahnke & Jenny Hosel for editing; my three lovely kids, Daniel, Amanda and Corlis; Renee Wing; JoAnn Caspar and Richard Ellis from the Clayton Historical Society; Jessica Boscacci & Milan Sikela; Steve B. and Chandra from the Clayton Club. I would like to thank Ms. Mann and Ms. Easton for being walking encyclopedias of Clayton area lore and for allowing me to pick their brains on many of the historic parts of the book. A thank you goes out to Ed Moresi and Peter Matheson for their insight; Pastor Sean for his tour of the old Pioneer building; and Mr. White for his help developing the book. Also, thanks to the Black Diamond Brewing Company for their input and splendid brews; Peter and Kristina at Cup O' Jo Coffee Shop for allowing me to spend so much time in their coffee shop; Kimberly H.; Abby, Katie and Sarah at the Royal Rooster; Tobi at Skipolini's Pizza; Shelley B. at Frontier Salon; Jeannie K and even though she was mentioned before, happy kisses to Jenny Hosel, my sweet lady, for putting up with me.

Richard Taylor thanked the following people in his notes: His family and friends, for their support and encouragement; his niece, who reportedly met the White Witch. In addition, he thanked Mike and Vernon, who saw the "mysterious visitor;" the people of Clayton; the City of Clayton; and Carl Graves, who shared his stories with Richard. He also wanted to thank The East Diablo Historical Association; Mt. Diablo Elementary School; Contra Costa Library System; The Black Diamond Regional Preserve; and Mount Diablo State Park.

INDEX:

Here are a litany of strange stories, all researched and entered into the following pages.

I beg of you to not bother any of the locations that are quoted in this book, but please visit the sites with your patronage and buy an item or two. Please be respectful of people's privacy and also the ability to run their businesses. I have spent months laying the ground work to contact these locations and most places do not want to be bothered with questions and people taking photos inside of their stores. PLEASE REFRAIN FROM THESE ACTIVITIES. Thank You.

If more details are needed, you may contact me and I will try to help.

1-Intro

Every town, village, hamlet and city in this country has its own set of folklore stories, UFO's, cryptozoology, hauntings, signs, and Native American stories. Many of these stories of the unexplained have been passed down over the years and through many generations. Many stories originated from eyewitnesses that swear what they saw was real or maybe from the minds of a person who had just one too many sips at the bar that night. These are stories that have made their way through generations and passed by word of mouth or in print. History dictates many stories; some of these stories may be true. Many times stories slightly change due to poor memory of the teller or the ability to make the stories just a tad more exciting to the listener.

So how do we come by these folklore stories in the first place? These were all researched from hand written notes in files from the museum, audio interviews of witnesses, dusty files in the basement of an old house, released government files, talking to the locals or scanned documents found on the micro-fiche in the library. These are all examples of what was claimed to be of so much importance at the time, that it was written down either typed or hand written for prosperity sake, and for me to study so many years later and put in book form.

Everyone grew up with tales of adventure or of the ghostly figures that hang out in the local woods. I am no exception to this rule. When in school in Swindon, England, we learned about the haunting of the local manors and stately homes. As I grew, I experienced strange things near my brother's home in Kent. These are all documented in my first book. *"What The Hell Was That. The trials and tribulations of an English ghost hunter in the USA."*

This book is a collection of well-known local tales as well as a lot of follow up and interviews with many local people during the early months of 2016. The details provided here all come from local people that have given me a basic story: and with the help of other locals, historians, libraries, locked away documents, the stories have made their way into this publication. As stated throughout this book, I am just the writer and I do not always believe in everything I am told or even see. Most of the people I interviewed regarding these official reports find themselves with a smirk on their faces and chuckle in their voice when telling me the stories that have come to them over the years. This is a book of folklore. It is a collection of accounts that have been passed down through many decades. Sometimes I have had to change the names of people and places and even omit names all together to protect locations, buildings and the personal space of the people telling me the stories. I want to protect the privacy of my sources as much as possible. A few of these stories would not have made this book if I had not agreed on changing names and locations. I had to agree to this privacy to get you; the reader, a full account of what happened.

So please sit back, relax with a warm beverage and read the accounts that have come out of this sleepy town called Clayton, California.

2 -How We Got To Clayton CA

After making my way West from Swindon, a large town one hour West of London, England back in 1986; I now find myself 30 years later, on the West coast of America staring out my office window at what was once a giant deposit of sedimentary rock from the ocean bed, and now has been carved by quarrying activities on the edge of Mt. Diablo.

After living a few years in San Leandro, California Jenny; who is the mother to my youngest child, decided to sell her house and move closer to her parents in Walnut Creek, so the search for a location began. Even though we had amazing neighbors and lived a very short walk to the water front in San Leandro, we packed up the house and moved out of a wonderful neighborhood. Gone were the days of walking to the San Francisco Bay and observing the wonderful view of the San Francisco skyline and the occasions of pushing "LBC" also known as "Little Baby Corlis" in her stroller along the coastline.

We found ourselves staying in a single bedroom

of the house of one of Jenny's friends. We were so grateful for the opportunity to have a room to ourselves, but we desperately needed for find a place of our own.

We searched on a daily basis; on the internet and on the streets, and seemed like we never would find a place that would work for us. The locations I loved, she did not. The places she loved, I was not fond of. We found a fantastic location that we both loved but then found out that it was in the breezeway of pollutants from the smoke stacks that lined the Delta. We found a wonderful location that we both loved, but the school system was not to the standard Jenny wanted for our daughter. Offers were made on homes, but the deals fell through.

Then one day we found a cute place in a community at the base of Mount Diablo in Contra Costa County, inland by about 45 minutes from the previous home we lived in. I had to take care of baby that day and I made a special point of getting her out of the house as much as possible. This day, I decided to take a trip over the hills and to a small town called Clayton. The area was like a diamond in the rough. Everyone was friendly throughout the old town community. It was as if we had stepped back in time to the 1960's when life was a lot simpler and people actually spoke to strangers. Upon my return to the one bedroom that we lived in, I mentioned our visit to Jenny and the rest is now history.

A deal was made and with the weeks of back and forth communications and heightened stress, we finally moved in and settled down. After weeks of moving boxes filled with our belongings and packing it all tightly into the two car garage, I started to look to the Historical Society for local history and lore of the area.

My fascination with history has made for many adventures and many more fun times during my life. I wanted this adventurous style to continue in our new location. The area of old Clayton is on the site of a mining community and many of the old buildings still remain. Most are now modern businesses like the Cup O' Jo coffee shop and the steak house. One of the original saloons still stands and is in full working order. The town is very small and it takes less than 20 minutes to walk the whole length and breadth of the community.

The town is dotted with historic markers that explain some of the history. There are stories of outlaws and prohibition; including the tales of "Robin Hood of the El Dorado" and the city founder, Joel Clayton's homestead. To my amazement, the locals were more than willing to share their stories with me and I was able to access many files and records regarding the area by just expressing what I wanted to do in creating a book about the lore of the town.

This book has been compiled from stories I have heard from the locals and from the huge amount of evidence that has been collected over the years from the town folk and historians of the area. All the stories entered into this book have been researched by me and with the help of many others we managed to publish this collection of events throughout the years of the small town called Clayton, California. To say all these stories are factual may be a stretch, but to the people that have reported these claims, they believe they saw what they saw and thought it important to report it.

Please read on and make of it whatever you wish but also, please remember I am just the messenger.

3- Dictionary Explanations

To make this book a little clearer to the general populous, here is a brief explanation of a few of the terms you will find within these pages. The text is taken from the Merriam – Webster dictionary online.

What is a Ghost?

Full Definition of *ghost* from Merriam – Webster dictionary:

A disembodied soul; *especially*: the soul of a dead person believed to be an inhabitant of the unseen world or to appear to the living in bodily likeness. i.e. a ghost - or spirit or apparition - is the energy, soul or personality of a person who has died and has somehow gotten stuck between this plane of existence and the next. Most researchers believe that these spirits do not know they are dead. Very often they have died under traumatic, unusual or highly emotional circumstances. Ghosts can be perceived by the living in a number of ways: through sight (apparitions), sound (voices), smell (fragrances and odors), touch - and sometimes they can just be sensed.

What is a Poltergeist?

Full Definition of *poltergeist* from Merriam – Webster dictionary:

A ghost that makes strange noises and causes objects to move. i.e. "Poltergeist" is a German word meaning "noisy spirit." Current research indicates, however, that poltergeist activity may have nothing to do with ghosts or spirits. Since the activity seems to center around an individual, it is believed that it is caused by the subconscious mind of that individual. It is, in effect, psychokinetic activity. The individual is often under emotional, psychological or physical stress.

What is Folklore?

Full Definition of *folklore* from Merriam – Webster dictionary:

Traditional customs, tales, sayings, dances, or art forms preserved among a people
a branch of knowledge that deals with folklore an often

unsupported notion, story, or saying that is widely circulated, i.e. The term folklore is generally used to refer to the traditional beliefs, myths, tales, and practices of a people which have been disseminated in an informal manner -- usually via word of mouth, although in modern times the Internet has become a pivotal source for folklore. The term folklore may also be used to define the comparative study of folk knowledge and culture.

The term "folklore" was first coined by William J. Thoms in 1846. Thoms was a British antiquarian who wanted a simple term to replace various awkward phrases floating around at the time to discuss the same concept; phrases such as "popular antiquities," the "lore of the people," and "the manners, customs, observances, superstitions, ballads, proverbs etc., of the olden times."

What are U.F.O.'s?

Full Definition of *U.F.O.s* from Merriam – Webster dictionary:

A flying object in the sky that some people believe could be a spaceship from another planet, i.e. Any object that flies and cannot initially be identified as an airplane, helicopter, blimp, balloon, kite, or any other object that normally flies, is a UFO. Many flying objects that are listed as a UFO can later be identified as an object made on Earth, then they can be called an "IFO," or identified flying object.

What is Cryptozoology?

Full Definition of *cryptozoology* from Merriam – Webster dictionary:

The study of and search for animals and especially legendary animals (as Sasquatch) usually in order to evaluate the possibility of their existence, i.e. Cryptozoology, which literally means "the study of hidden animals," is one of the newest life sciences, and certainly one of the most exciting. During the last half-century, interest in sightings and traditions dealing with "monsters" has moved from a shadowy world of travelogues to academic respectability and beyond.

What is a Legend?

Full Definition of *Legend* from Merriam – Webster dictionary:

A story from the past that is believed by many people, but cannot be proved to be true or a famous or important person who is known for doing something extremely well, i.e. *Legend* has several related meanings. A legend today may be someone of noted celebrity, with larger-than-life accomplishments, whose fame is well-known. Another meaning of this word is a literary genre. In this capacity, the term is much-abused, used synonymously with *myth*, *tall tale*, and *history*. However, it makes more sense to use the term *legend* — as it is, in fact, often used — to name a type of literature that falls somewhere between myth, tall tales, and history and that otherwise has no name.

4- A Brief History of Clayton CA

In 1857, the town of Clayton was laid out and founded by Joel Henry Clayton (1812–1872) and his two younger brothers. Clayton was born in Bugsworth, now Buxworth, in the United Kingdom, and immigrated to the United States in 1837. Joel was a Scotland #1 Knight of the Templar and later became a 33 degree Mason, he had the honor of being the first person in California to earn this level. After many years in other states, he settled down with his wife Margaret (1820–1908) at his town at the foot of Mt. Diablo, where he and his family prospered. Clayton was named after Joel Henry Clayton, although literally it was only by the 'flip of a coin.' Joel Clayton and Charles Rhine co-founded the town, and each wanted to name it after himself. If Charles had won it would have become Rhinesville, but Joel Clayton won. Joel and his wife Margaret both died in Clayton, and were buried in Live Oak Cemetery in what is now Concord, CA. Clayton was a hub of activity during the height of the coal mines in the area and was the central location for the miner's recreation and relaxation.

For people who have never been to this delightful town of Clayton, here is a description of what it is like to walk through the old town area. As you come off of the new bypass road that runs past the town, you enter what was once the main road that ran through the center of town. You arrive in what looks like an old Wild West town. The sidewalks are cast in concrete with the pattern of an old boardwalk. Many of the old buildings have been replaced with period style structures. You walk down the main street and notice that the streets are lined with trees that are full and welcoming. It creates a feeling of calm and you can take a seat on one of many benches that line this 2 block area. At the far end is a newer play park, a large patch of grass, and a couple of gazebos. This was once a eucalyptus grove way before modernization. There remains one tavern that looks like it is right out of a Western movie. Then across the street are a few original homes from the early days of the town, now converted into the Historical Society. The town has a small grocery store, a dog grooming shop, hair salon, Dentist office, church, steak house, pizza and sub shops, and an amazing bocce ball court located near the entrance to the town.

As you look upwards you will see the mountain rising in the distance and the rolling hills on the other side of the city. Even though the area has been in a drought and the hills show a tone of yellow; after rains, the wonderful shades of green are seen on the hillside. Cattle roam and appear to be ant sized due to the vastness of the surroundings. The clouds surround the mountain top with a beautiful blue sky behind it.

I have had the honor of meeting the local residents who have all helped me with these stories. Many of the stories were told at the actual locations of the folklore. Most of these follow up details have come from the Clayton Historical Society.

5- The Haunting at the Clayton Club

Clayton's oldest and continuously operated

business is now known as The Clayton Club Saloon. Originally named The Rhine Hotel, it was built by Jacob Rhine circa 1873. Jacob operated the Hotel/Saloon and ice cream parlor at the corner of Main and Morris Streets in Clayton from 1874 – 1898 after it was gutted by fire and rebuilt by Jacob Rhine once more. In 1898, the saloon was renamed and called The National Saloon. This popular saloon has continuously served the public and survived Prohibition and the Great Depression years.

In 1905, Carl Berendsen added a building at the rear of the structure that he had shipped from San Francisco to Martinez and then transported to Clayton by horse and wagon. This rear area served as a kitchen and a residence for the family for many years, while the front portion of the building was used as a saloon as well as a restaurant and the family's home, until Prohibition in the 1920s. From 1920-1933 the Clayton Club survived as a café, renamed the Clayton Café, and Social Club. During this prohibition period the Clayton Café offered non-alcoholic drinks, meals and entertainment, or so we are told and lead to believe.

Entering this bar is like stepping back in time to the period of the coal miners and the wild-west days. The bar appears to be original with a large mirror in the center of the decorative carved dark woodwork. The ceiling tiles are stained brown from many years of smoke build up from the times when smoking was an accepted past-time, way before health was anything to worry about. The floors between the additions and the main building are slightly uneven and the boards creek when you walk on them. The feeling of being drunk can be achieved by just walking the length of the bar due to the slant of the floors that cause you to sway from side to side as you go. Raw wooden panels line many of the walls and show the original layout of the building before they expanded to allow more space and more patrons. The smell of years of cigarette smoke has worked its way into the woodwork and adds character.

The walls are covered with images of cowboys, wranglers and stock men from all eras. Most of the pictures are framed in wood and are screwed to the walls so as not to be knocked down by the many regulars that make their way to their seats and bump this narrow corner of the historic saloon. Glowing brightly, neon lights with catchy logos and corporate imagery, give a strange hue to small areas throughout the bar. The neon glow causes an onslaught for your attention in your peripheral vision when you face the bar; seated on one of the well worn four legged bar stools that line the length of the bar. The saloon itself is a very dark place with very few windows to let the daylight pass in. For the first timers that make their way to this establishment, the saloon appears very much like it did over 100 years ago. The saloon is divided into two sections; separated by a partition, with the main area that houses the bar at the front and a smaller dance floor and sitting area in the back of the saloon.

Plaques with words of wisdom are scattered throughout the building. An array of framed images and historic artifacts adorn this famous watering hole wherever you glance. A couple of signs that I found rather entertaining were the steel plate that states *"Good Cowgirls Keep Their Calves Together"* and *"Cowboys, Leave Your Gun at the Bar."* Old keys, cow roping equipment, and Indian artifacts hang throughout the place, giving patrons a constant reminder that they have not just entered a bar, but they have stepped back in history. There is a feeling that the spirits of many dead cowboys still haunt the establishment. Memories of days gone by are molded into the walls, floors and paneling throughout.

With all the cowboy memorabilia around, one item seems very much out of place. There is a child's wooden sled mounted on the wall at a slight angle occupies an area at the rear of the location. It is hard to see if you were not looking for it, as it blends into the bare wood paneling. It has faded red paintwork and shiny runners and it sits, mounted firmly on the wall. It seems an odd fit for a saloon decoration, it seems better suited to the museum across the street.

With the exception of the neon signs and two televisions mounted within the bar area, there is one other item that gives away the fact we are living in the 2010's. There is a very impressive jukebox that is mounted along one wall right behind the seated area near the bar. The jukebox lights up and with the crispness of any high definition television showing images of some of the more modern music artists of the day; but 9 times out of 10, all you hear coming out of this ultra modern device, is classic country and western tunes with the occasional heavy rock of the seventies and if you are really lucky you may catch a tune from the 2000's. This style of western music just adds to the charm of this old time saloon. You may catch yourself singing along with songs you have not heard in years. It is not unheard of for the people scattered throughout the building to start singing with whatever is being played on the jukebox. This adds to the atmosphere of friendly comfort that this place holds in the hearts of the locals. To vouch for this statement, I know that I often join in singing during a few of the old classics from the likes of Cash, Jennings, Skynard and Seger.

During the early morning hours, you will find Steve; the owner of the Clayton Club, wandering around the bar; many times sporting an impressive Stetson hat, assisting with maintenance, ordering supplies and making store runs for odds and ends such as lemons and limes for the fancier cocktails that are mixed here. Steve was one of the people that helped me the most with the venture into the folklore of the area. He is an encyclopedia of knowledge about Clayton and he is dedicated to preserving this knowledge with artifacts and folklore for public viewing within the bar and by collecting as much information as possible. The items throughout his bar create a feeling of a living museum.

The heads of deer hang on the walls as trophies to the conquering of these poor beasts somewhere in the surrounding hills and valleys. They now collect dust and stare off into space as if looking into the past, prior to when the rough and tumble days of the Wild West made way for the enjoyable watering hole that exists today. I encourage anyone that reads this book to at least venture in for a quick drink and take in this amazing location ripe with history and nostalgia.

My newest buddy and fellow Anglican, sits in a corner of the bar with his newspaper and his cup of coffee every day of the week. I often sit with him and chat about social issues and news events that are relevant at that moment in time. In this corner I recently noticed an old safe with the inscription that states "Dyeing Works – California Cleaning" It appears this safe holds it secrets, as it looks like the combination remains intact and it has not been opened in years.

Tucked into the very corner of the saloon, with full view of any activity that may take place is what is known as the Library corner. It is a book rack filled with romantic novels and books of no importance in this modern day and age. The books mainly collect dust with the exception of a couple of written literature pieces that have now found a new use within this building. Due to my English friend's background as a retired college professor, he is known to select two books, of no interest to him, to help cover the air conditioning vent that is located under his feet. He positions the books in such a way to deflect the blast of cold air that rises right under his seat. The two books of further education and now wind deflectors are titled *"A Guide to Harvard Law"* and *"Letters of acceptance to Harvard."* When asked why these particular books are used to prevent his chilling, he responded that these books are worthless and make a great deflector of the cold. It appears there is more respect for corny love novels than the works of this well known institution of advanced learning.

The Clayton Club is well known for their unique way of honoring the fallen cowboys of the Clayton area. The Clayton Club honors its dead by hanging a pair of the deceased cowboy's boots from the ceiling. Each set of boots has the name of the departed inscribed with white paint on the soles. There is also a plaque that hangs on the wall commemorating the passing of many other patrons. Once a year, there is a ceremony to honor the fallen and to remember the stories of these amazing characters. This is the only time the strict rule of *"No one under the age of 21 allowed"* is relaxed and the locals gather to pay their respects to family and friends. The saloon takes on a whole different feeling once the place is emptied out of revelers and party folk late at night.

All the neon lights are extinguished, the jukebox is turned off and the doors are bolted firmly shut with the help of many locking devices. This is the time when paranormal activities start to take place in the bar. Paranormal activity is not a daily thing here, but when it does happen, it is made clear to anyone that is willing to listen. So starts the first paranormal folklore activity of the famous Clayton Club Saloon.

It has been reported that on one occasion, during a cleanup period in the empty bar, the remaining staff members felt what was described as a cold breeze. The experience was a short blast of frigid air and not a wind blowing through the building. It was enough for the bartender to stop in his tracks and try to mentally register what was going on around him. Something then caught his eye and as he glanced skywards he noticed one pair of cowboy boots that was mounted on the ceiling, start to spin on its mounting hook. It started slowly but then the boots started to spin faster. The boots turned back and forth as if some invisible entity was physically pushing them. Then out of the blue the boots stopped spinning as if someone had grabbed them with their clenched hand, preventing any form of movement. It was enough to cause severe concern on behalf of the bar keeper and even though he had no belief in ghosts, he too departed the premises as quickly as possible that night.

The story was shared the next day and with the help of friends, they saw no earthly way these boots would spin on their own then come to an abrupt halt. Everyone wanted to put the spinning of the boots down to an earthquake or the wind blowing through the building, but if that were the case, other items in the bar would have moved too.

As in many haunted buildings throughout the World, Clayton Club Saloon can add the, oh so popular, 'heavy footsteps walking in the attic area' story to the collection of lore in their dedicated drinking establishment. So the story goes, it was a few years back when the morning staff, including a maintenance man and cleaners, attended to their daily duties in the building, when one person behind the bar heard what was thought to be the sound of a co-worker walking around above them in the attic space. Thinking nothing of it, the bar maid continued to work on her tasks. The footsteps continued and at one point all three members of staff were all standing in view of each other in the area near the bar. The group instinctively looked up to try and figure out what they were hearing. All stood silently and pointed to try to locate the spot where the heavy steps were coming from. The footsteps were heavy enough to be tracked across the length of the attic and then with a shuffle the footsteps would return to the spot that they started. Then it went silent as if the person in the attic has decided to take a seat and relax or if the aforementioned decided to stand still for a very long time. There were no more steps, and the building went quiet once more.

The maintenance man decided to go and find out who was in the attic space and who was making all that noise above them. The entrance to the attic area was in clear view of the staff and there was no one descending the stairs during this whole time. The maintenance man climbed the steps and lifted the trap door to the attic space. The brave soul slowly disappeared above ceiling level and only his boots were visible on the top rung of the ladder. His boots finally disappeared into the ceiling and the exact same sound was heard as he moved from one corner to the other corner in the attic. The same volume and density to the steps were heard moving around above the others heads. As before when all three of them heard the sounds, the two workers tracked the footsteps and could visualize where the man was at any given time. The steps were heard returning to the door opening and they witnessed him descending back to ground level. With a look of amazement, he said there was no one up there and with a look of confusion, shuffled over and took a seat at the bar. What was there to say? Was it a ghost or were all three of them imagining things?

Back in June 20, 2012, a news article was published in the "Claycord News" that asked "*The Historic Clayton Club – Is it Haunted?*" The text continued *"A Claycordian recently sent this photo, along with the information below….*

This picture was taken a while back at the Clayton Club. I sent it to a few people and now I hear it's spreading like a virus. There seems to be what appears to be a ghost of an old bearded man above the passed out man. Now people have pointed out what appears to be something creepy peeking out behind the post under the yellow sign (left bottom).

Someone else is having it blown up and printed and wants to look at old Clayton pics to see if it resembles anyone. What do you think???

Claycordians, tell us what you think!"

Some of the responses were not positive or that of believers.

- *It's called a dirty camera lens…*

- *If you zoom in to the picture you can see it's a cowboy boot with a reflection of either the flash or the light coming from the right.*

- *I do believe in spirits, and I know the CC is pretty old (late 1800's?), not surprising…. not sure if that is what is in this picture but it wouldn't surprise me at all. Just wish the spirits would buy a round of drinks for us!*

On the other hand you have these posts that truly believe there is something in that building.

Posted letters went on to say:

- *That's Doug Mitchell, or the ghost of him anyway. He was a first generation Claytonian who's parents were original settlers of the area. Mitchell Canyon bears their name.*

- *Doug Mitchell's house was in the eucalyptus grove where the Village Grocery is now. He died in mid-1970s, just a year or two after the house burned down.*
  The Clayton Club is just across the street from Doug's residence, and apparently he still enjoys visiting the place. Who wouldn't? Particularly with all them prowlin' 50 year old ladies!

- *oh heck yeah... I believe it's haunted. Along with the building the Clayton museum. There's some "interesting" energy in those buildings. Pretty much any of the old buildings in Clayton have some sort of paranormal activity going on, and*

not necessarily in that creepy Hollywood
portrayal.

http://claycord.com/2012/06/20/the-historic-clayton-club-is-it-haunted/

Give the place a visit and make up your own mind.

6- Clayton's Orange Ball of Light

It was the early 2000's and two days after people across the West coast of the United States reported seeing a mysterious streak of light traveling across the morning sky. No one had been able to explain what it could have been as it was clearly not that of an airplane or a helicopter. The mysterious streak of light was observed at around 6 am on a Friday morning by various people in and around Clayton, CA. There were reports of people seeing the same streak of light in Oregon, as well as Nevada, according to a report by *NBC News*.

"While astronomers have started researching the source of the light, there has been no confirmed explanation for the phenomenon two days after the witnessed event." According to one of the eyewitness reports, the mysterious streak of light was definitely not that of an aircraft. The witness tells Claycord News and Talk; *"I am used to seeing planes early in the morning with lights, but this was different. This had something coming out of it, it wasn't just the light. I could see it spraying something."*

It was not just one person who affirmed that the object emitted something as it streaked through the early morning sky. Here is an eyewitness account of another person who also confirmed seeing the same streak of light, as told to *WND*.

"This morning when I was leaving for work,

before I got into my car, I noticed that there was some type of object in the air with a type of floodlight on, and white fog/smoke was billowing out of it – as if something was being sprayed into the air. I tried to take a photo with my iPhone but it didn't come out. This was at 5:58 am and the object appeared to be just over the area of Clayton Valley Shopping Center at Clayton/Kirker Pass. I was a bit concerned because the object was clearly spraying some substance into the air with the floodlight on. Then the light went off, and I couldn't see or hear the sounds from a plane or anything, it was very strange."

Another account came from a Clayton resident and in his words, according to what was aired on local TV Station *KPIX-TV:*

"About 6 a.m. this morning, I came out, I was walking down the driveway and I looked up at the sky and saw this little orange ball – above the Redwood trees. All of a sudden these lights just came down from that little orange ball."

While it is natural for the everyday person to be baffled by this mysterious streak of light in the sky, this time even astronomers and seasoned weathermen seem to have no clue what it could have been. According to staff members that work at the Chabot Space and Science Center in Oakland, CA, they had no confirmation as to what the object could have been. The staff member told the *San Francisco Chronicle*, *"It may be space junk, it may be a meteor, but we have no confirmation yet. We're just kind of going off what we're getting from viewers and e-mail and video."*

Bob Benjamin, who works as a National Weather Service Forecaster, was also baffled as to what the mysterious streak of light could have been. *"There's, as far as I know, no meteorological phenomena associated with that,"* he told the San Francisco Chronicle.

To make things even more bizarre, the U.S. Air Force which conducts missile tests at the Vandenberg Air Force Base, located 9.2 miles northwest of Lompoc, California, and a five hour drive from Clayton, have said that there was no missile launch on that Friday morning and no military activity from any other bases in the area. The air space was reported clear the day this mysterious streak of light was seen burning up the skies. The lack of a cohesive explanation to the reports of this mysterious streak of light has led to several theories being talked about through paranormal groups, conspiracy theorist and aviation groups. Some people say it could have been an UFO, while others have raised concerns over the lack of air security over the U.S. skies. Conspiracy theorists say that a form of chemical testing was taking place on the people of the area with a controlling chemical released from mystery planes.

The story was never proven one way or the other, and now just sits as part of the Clayton area folklore.

7- The Little Old Man on the Hill

Located on a hilltop that overlooks Ygnaico Valley Road is the final resting place of many of the early pioneers and local explorers of the area. There is a small grave site that is invisible from the road, but if you know where to look, you will find the shattered remains of headstones and other markers jutting up from the hardened soil. Modern paving stones and mulch are now laid in place and a brand new gate with a huge lock secures the site from any form of vandalism. The large oak trees offer shade from the scorching California summer sun as the ground slowly bakes under temperatures over one hundred degrees. Clayton's founder; Joel Clayton, lies here in an unmarked grave along with other local pioneer families like the Babels, Atchinsons, Denkingers, Duncans, Franks, Mitchells, and the Treats, just to name a few. A historic plaque now rests in the graveyard as a memorial to this location's historic past.

The cemetery lies on the corner of the Rancho Morte del Diablo land grant and later was donated to the community of Clayton by the Pacheco family. This family owned most of the Pleasant Hill/Concord area during the early days of Spanish settlement. There was only one stipulation connected to the passing of ownership and that was that the cemetery would be opened for the burial of Spanish families that lived in the area and helped the region to grow and flourish.

There have been many changes to the way the

cemetery could be accessed over the years. It now lies in the center of land development and housing projects and is rather difficult to find.

Over the years, many people have reported seeing a little old man with a bouquet of flowers wandering around the monuments and headstones at all hours of the day and night. He walks slowly around the stones with his head held low and with no emotion upon his ashen face. Everyone that has reported a sighting claims he wears a dusty old fashioned dark double breasted suit. He has been seen talking to young children and young children appear to be drawn to him when he is seen. But when any adult makes an effort to communicate or approach his whittled old frame, he disappears into thin air. It appears to eye witnesses that it looks like he has a bouquet of flowers for his loved one (maybe his deceased wife) but he appears to be unable to find her grave site. He wanders as if he is lost and is searching desperately for a loved one. This agonizing image of great sadness has been reported on many occasions. The spirit is harmless and appears to be what is called an intelligent spirit, which means he is able to interact and recognize children from adults. No name has ever been associated with him and there is no record of his grave at this site. The owners and operators of this location have not heard this story before, but say that there is a distinct possibility it may be true.

(Note-the name of the cemetery has been withheld due to an increase in graveyard vandalism over the past 15 years).

8- Joaquin Murietta: Bandit of the Goldfields – Clayton's Robin Hood

A California Outlaw Story retold by S.E. Schlosser.

Joaquin Murietta and wife Rosita lived with his older brother Carlos in the Clayton area. The three Mexican immigrants were living on a small, successful farm before trying their hand in the gold fields. However, the other miners living nearby tried to run them off, telling them that it was illegal for Mexicans to pan for gold or hold a claim anywhere near the gold fields North of Clayton. The Murietta brothers ignored their threats and continued to live peacefully on their farm and work in the gold-fields.

Enraged by this flagrant disregard for the American laws, a drunken mob attacked the little family late one night, shooting Carlos, and then raping and murdering Rosita while Joaquin was forced to watch. The mob bound the Mexican to a stake in the yard, where they beat him with a whip. He strained angrily against his bonds, but finally his wounds overcame him and he slumped senseless against the post. The mob left him for dead, but when a few sober citizens came the next day to help the Mexican family, Joaquin had disappeared.

A few months later, a dark-bearded, long-haired stranger with cold black eyes set up a gambling establishment in Hangtown. Shortly after the stranger's arrival in town, miners started going missing, one after another, and their dead bodies were turning up in unlikely places. All of them had their ears cut off. A few of the smarter folks realized that each of the dead miners had been a party to the illegal slaying of Carlos and Rosita Murietta. There were thirty-one men in the mob that night, and fourteen were now dead. When this became known, the other seventeen men scattered to the winds overnight; but one by one, they were hunted down, killed, and their ears were cut off.

Finally, a miner who had once had a claim near to the Murietta brothers came to Hangtown and identified the owner of the gambling establishment as Joaquin Murietta. His cover blown, the Mexican fled into the wilds and started to gather other wild and restless Mexicans to him. Soon he was the head of a mighty gang, riding a black stallion and robbing the Americans of their gold. Dangling from the bandit's saddle was the string of dried ears taken from the members of the mob who killed his wife and brother. Together with his bandits, Joaquin Murietta robbed the miners of a million dollars in gold. Yet for all his ruthlessness, Joaquin was kind to his fellow Mexicans, and never turned down a friend in need. He gave his riches liberally to the poor, and avenged those who were oppressed. In return, they sheltered him from the law, and called blessings down upon him.

Travel in the goldfields was made nearly

impossible by the threat of Joaquin Murietta and his gang, so California's governor hired a group of rangers to track down and kill Joaquin. Led by Captain Love, the rangers ambushed Joaquin and his men, and shot the Mexican bandit and his horse to death. Captain Love decapitated the Mexican bandit and put his head into a jar filled with alcohol, which he paraded through the streets of San Francisco. The head was finally placed behind the bar of the Golden Nugget Saloon in San Francisco; where it leered at the folks who came there to drink until the saloon was destroyed in the 1906 earthquake.

   To this day, Joaquin's headless ghost continues to ride through the gold fields, terrorizing all who cross his path with cries of: "Give me back my head."

   Clayton has a historic marker dedicated to Murrieta that sits outside of the Clayton Historical Society building states *"Born in Mexico in 1832 the renowned "Robin Hood of the El Dorado" spent his early days in California working in Contra Costa County as a vaquero before turning bandit."*
Dedicated By

Joaquin Murrieta Chapter No. 13
E Clampus Vitus
November 6, 1976 in Commemoration
of our Bicentennial Year"

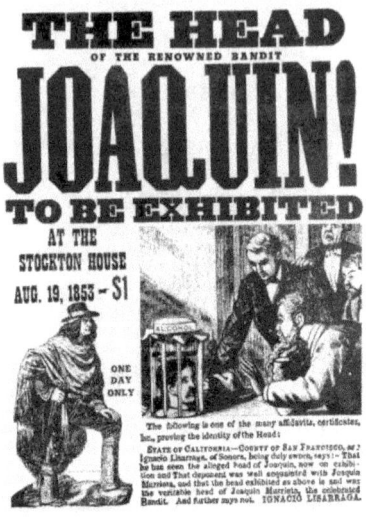

Legend has it that in 1919 Johnston McCulley received his inspiration for his fictional character Don Diego de la Vega better known as Zorro from the 1854 book entitled *The Life and Adventures of Joaquin Murrieta, The Celebrated California Bandit* by John Rollin Ridge. John heard about a Mexican miner who had turned to banditry and was intrigued by the story.

9 - On A Collision Course

This account was submitted through AVCAT (Aviation Catalog). AVCAT is a special project being conducted by NICAP (The National Investigations Committee On Aerial Phenomena) with the help and cooperation of the original compiler of AIRCAT (UFO file and documenting system), Dr. Richard Haines and other sources, to create a comprehensive listing of sightings from aircraft with detailed documentation from these sources, including Projects SIGN, GRUDGE & BLUE BOOK.

Released government papers read as follows: "*On Feb. 20, 1952, while flying above Mt. Diablo, just South of Clayton, California in a military aircraft B-25, Captain John Watkins (pilot) and Captain Richard Montgomery (co-pilot) of B-25 #8820, observed a bright yellow light ahead of them, between Stockton and Sacramento, California, while flying the aircraft at 8,000 feet. It was reported that an object approached at a very high speed right in front of the plane and passed within collision distance. The pilot stated that the object was definitely not another aircraft and he was unsure of what it could have been. The object first came into view on an apparent collision course with the B-25. No other aircraft in the area & no radar returns were witnessed. To follow up on this sighting, a request for information was sent to AFB McClellan, Travis, Hamilton, Castle and AFB Moffett military bases for more information on air traffic at that time. Their reports all came back negative of any aircraft or balloons in the area at the time specified in the inquiry. Radar in surrounding areas picked up the image of the B-25, but radar never showed any other object within the vicinity during the alleged interaction. Released government documents state the plane just finished a radar bomb drop near a range in Pittsburg, California. It was on its return, on a course of 82% when the plane prepared for a turn to 72% towards Stockton California, when the bright yellow ball came into sight."* The official Air Intelligence Information Report; that was made public in 1968, states *"Pilots sighted what they first believed to be a plane with only one (1) landing light on, or a bright light on the nose. Object first appeared to be between Stockton and Sacramento, California. As the object approached the aircraft, it appeared to get larger and brighter and more yellow in color. As the object passed in front of the observing aircraft, the pilot stated it defiantly was not another aircraft."* The comment note at the bottom of the document adds some validation to this claim as it is written, *"No physical evidence is available (fragments or photographs) to confirm sighting. Both are rated pilots with a good amount of flying experience. The evaluation of this report is twofold as another aircraft reported the sighting of this object."*

This was just another unexplained UFO incident above the City of Clayton, CA. Is there a reason for all this mountain top activity? Could it be closely related to the military air force bases that are scattered throughout the area? We may never know the answer to these questions.

10 - Seminary Night Visitors

The story goes that during the early 1990s, on

the knoll near March Creek Road, stood an old run down building that; at one time, was reported to be a seminary for young men to prepare for ordination as clergy or for other ministry work. The Claretian Brothers of Los Angeles vacated the premises, but the old buildings remained in use until it was torn down in 2006. With overgrown grass and weeds, the place was in serious need of repair and many of the buildings had started to deteriorate. The area returned to the wilderness with nature reclaiming it with the exception of one building that was still occupied. This building was the old caretaker's home that was now being rented to an area family. Over the years, the surrounding area was developed for future home expansion of the area at the base of the mountain.

The last remaining occupied house was notified that they were obligated to move out and allow the developers to pull down their home to make way for more modern buildings.

The remaining family was that of the former head master and his wife along with their children. Due to the amount of time, effort, sweat and tears that this family had put into making the school work for so many years, they were not willing to back down to a mega corporation and just buckle and move out. They decided to take drastic action and stay put for as long as possible as a sign of protest. The land developer was not pleased with the family and sent out a letter of eviction. The family hunkered down and held their ground. The decision was made to start turning off the utilities to the area as this was holding up development of the land. Times started to get more and more difficult once the power was shut off and the family was plunged into darkness every night and cold chill filled the air. The discomfort was not enough to break the will of the family and they stayed put with more intensity than ever before. At night, the house was lit with camping lanterns and they cooked over a camp stove, just to survive.

This was not just about the family moving from the location to make way for new homes. This was more about the way they were told to move and the removal of what the headmaster had created. He felt as if his years of work were for naught and he was just in the way of mindless land development.

After a short period of time living in darkness, the lanterns would start going out without any warning. The lanterns were seen rocking back and forth on their bases. Then there was the feeling of frigid spots in certain locations within the house, but nowhere else in the room would these spots be felt. This was put down to the wind blowing through the now dilapidated window panels.

With all these strange happenings, things started to get scary for the family when they had an experience that shook them to the core. One late night, after the family had met with the developers, it was discussed that they were not moving out no matter what actions were taken by the company. On returning to the home and settling in for the night. During the early hours of the morning the young lad of the family woke up and proceeded to the kitchen to get a drink of water. Everyone else was sleeping, but the thirsty son glanced out of the window while chugging a glass of water and saw two men standing at the fence line in what appeared to be a motionless stance. At this point the son was in a panicked state and rushed back into the bedroom to wake his father, as he thought the contractors were there to cause the family harm. The father jumped up and ran to the window to witness this strange sight that stood a few feet before him. Peering through the pane of glass, they watched as the figures turned in unison and slowly moved down the fence line. They appeared to float and held their balance as they crossed the uneven ground toward the new parking lot that was recently constructed on part of the old school site. The two images were young men wearing long sleeved white shirts, one slightly taller than the other. The father decided he was going to investigate.

He quickly unlocked the back door and grabbed a blunt object then he stepped outside to confront the unwanted intruders. The figures turned and started to encroach on the homeowner's property once more. The faces were blank and they stared off into space as if they had no idea who was in front of them or as if they were in a deep trance. The headmaster prepared for a confrontation; but to his horror, the two people that stood within ten feet of him both vanished into thin air.

They just disappeared right before his eyes without even a trace of there ever being anyone there. He was left alone with just pitch black darkness all around him. The feeling of shock swept over the man and he dropped to his knees and started to pray. Slowly rising from his knees, he made his way back into the homestead. Not saying a word to anyone so not to alarm his family and then he returned to his bed. He did not sleep the rest of the night due to the images racing through his mind, over and over again.

What were the images of the two men that night? Were they former students of the seminary or were they the ghosts of people that once lived on the property that was now new houses and a parking lot? No one will ever know. The building was finally demolished in February of 2006 and replaced with new housing on the ever expanding Clayton. The spirits have not been reported since.

The former caretaker / manager could not verify this story in her final five years of working at this location.

11- Frog in the Sandstone

Fate Magazine wrote an article on a very rare find straight up the hillside from our humble abode here in Clayton.

Coal is a strange place to find a living animal but a live frog was found by some workmen engaged in sinking a vertical shaft at the Black Diamond Coal Company's mine close to Mount Diablo, near Clayton CA. In 1873 a rock was found 172 feet below the surface, embedded in solid sandstone. A partial imprint and perfect outline of a frogs form was left upon the rock where it was found. The rock was gently removed and then the stone was broken open to find the most amazing sight ever, a live frog. The animal lived for twelve hours after its extraction, having very possibly been injured in the process of removal.

The president of the coal company was said to have later presented the remains to the San Francisco Academy of Sciences. But with a recent report from the San Francisco Academy of Sciences Contact Center representative, this artifact is no longer on display and they show no record of it being in their database. They are now intrigued by this story I have brought to their attention and now they are willing to track the legend further. So where has the frog in the stone gone? It continues to amaze and puzzle anyone who hears the story.

12-The Legend of Richard Taylor

When I decided that I was going to write a book about local folklore in and around Clayton, I noticed that most of the stories had been already reviewed or written by many people in many media forms. One of the main writers was a local man by the name of Richard Taylor.

Everywhere I went, I heard the name Richard Taylor mentioned, but no one knew what had become of him over the last year but everyone knew Richard was not in the area any more. Richard was a historian for the City of Clayton and a teacher of history in the local school system. Over thirty years ago, before the paranormal craze took off and every town has someone wanting to make it big on TV, Mr. Taylor formed a "Ghost Walk." This was an event that would take place around the Halloween period. Mr. Taylor would dress in Victorian period attire and walk with a candle lit lamp in hand.

The tours started out as a way of sharing local history with a group of school kids but rapidly moved into a much bigger task than Richard ever thought it would ever be. He had no idea how many people would show after a Friday night football game that coincided with his inaugural event. It was also a cold night so he was not sure many folks would want to walk around town after a cold night sitting in the bleachers at the football game. To his delight, there were a fair amount of people that showed up and with the help of his niece who handed out treats, they visited twelve paranormal locations on this first ever ghost walk. Stories were shared and the walk itself was a short one as the town is only three blocks long. Just enough time to keep the interest of his listeners and to get everyone home at a reasonable hour.

Mr. Taylor was happy with the outcome of his

first event and returned to his normal duties in the community with a feeling of success in his heart. The following years, Richard was contacted by the local press about his tour and what he had to offer. The interview was conducted and Richard prepared for the upcoming event as he had in the years past.

With an hour or so to go before everyone met at Endeavor Hall in Clayton, he had a feeling this was going to be a big night for him. It was clear that the story in the paper had sparked a lot of interest as the cars kept flooding into the old town Clayton area. All available parking spots were quickly filled and Richard had to rapidly recruit friends to help park the mass of vehicles full of folks wanting to join the paranormal tour. With rain coming down, Richard assigned a "puddle patrol" and a couple of friends set up a make shift intercom system so Richard could be heard by everyone in attendance.

The reaction to the tour was very positive. It was very popular due to the entertaining speaker and the ability to complete the walk in a rather short period of time. As years before it was just long enough to hold the attention of the masses that had showed up.

The success of the tour was a delight to Richard and his friends. The following years' reaction was not expected at all.

Very much like the year before, Richard received a phone call from an area newspaper, but this time it was the San Francisco Chronicle wanting a story for their biggest selling Sunday edition. There was no gauge on the expected turn out. All that was said to Mr. Taylor was that the story would run a week before his event. The paper printed the story and the phone calls started flooding in.

The newspaper story generated huge interest and over five hundred people descended on the sleepy town for this short tour with many of the folks promising to return the following year. The event was growing in leaps and bounds from year to year. The next year a theatrical element was added when a local decided he was going to depict the "headless horseman" with sparks flying off the black horse's custom made titanium horse shoes. It was a thrilling sight to behold and the crowd loved this additional element of surprise.

The show kept growing and one year it included an appearance of Sarah "Granny" Norton in her white dress and shroud handing out pamphlets promoting the Black Diamond Regional Preserve. There were "Ghost Sightings" at the end of Main Street when two cloaked figures appeared from over the brow of the hill on the South end of town near the City Corral. To top off the craziness of the event, as the group approached one of the local taverns and a young lady popped out in a playboy bunny suit, inviting everyone in for "Some Fun!"

So how much further could this tour go? The following year included the appearance of the ghost of Murrieta with white powdered face and black eyes accompanied by a huge explosion to introduce the entity. The gunpowder used may have been a little excessive as the whole down town area rocked from the blast.

The tours continued for many more years until the City decided that the increased use of police time took away from all the other community activities and they asked Richard to stop the walks.

After the walks stopped, Richard R. Taylor disappeared from the public eye. Memories of his famous ghost walk started to fade with outsiders, but remained strong with the locals. In recent years, Richard fell on hard times and no longer lives in the Clayton area. Many attempts were made to find Mr. Taylor and were met with disconnected phone lines, and dead e-mail addresses. Even knocking on the doors of his last known residence was fruitless. It appeared Mr. Taylor had disappeared just like the legends he wrote about back in 1992.

As I was sitting in my office looking out over Mt. Diablo and finishing up a section of this book, Jenny brought my phone to me and said it was for me. I answered and the voice came back saying "Hello this is Richard Taylor." Finally, Richard was found. He may have vanished from the public eye in Clayton, but he was still in the county. I had a long conversation with him and he confirmed my stories and added more details that I had not heard before. For example, he appeared on a television show called "Sightings" in the early 1990's; the forerunner show to the current television paranormal craze. He said that he had a long conversation with executive producer, Henry Winkler (who was an actor on the show "Happy Days and played "The Fonz"). As of the writing of this book, I heard that Mr. Taylor moved on to other communities to offer ghost walks. Richard Taylor is one of the reasons many of these stories live today, and for that I thank him.

13-The White Witch Tale

Every city has a tale of a White Witch. Many of these come with a long line of folklore connected to them.

The Clayton area seems to have two stories about two different people. This could be due to a true story mixing with folklore building over the years. The facts on Sarah "Granny" Norton have been researched and proven to be factual. The validity of the hauntings will be left up to the readers.

Even though Sarah Norton was not buried in Clayton, the unfortunate incidents that lead to her demise were very much related to the small town of

Clayton.

The story of the woman who is known as the White Witch of Nortonville is one of the more popular folklore stories in the area. This is a tall tale of witchcraft followed by a more realistic story to follow. Full credit for the writing goes to Andrea Allison on Thursday, April 19, 2007 who penned the following story.

The story goes:

Black Diamond started as a coal mining town in the 1800's. Now, it is considered a ghost town inhabited by two spirits, Mary and Sarah, that share the same nickname.

There are conflicting stories about Mary; I personally

believe the second one. The first states she was hired by a family to be their nanny, but she didn't disclose to her employers that she practiced witchcraft. When they found out, they immediately fired her. The next day she was found dead in the mines. How she died is still unknown.

The other story has her as the one that looked after all the children in the town of Nortonville. Then, all the children died suddenly of mysterious illnesses. The town quickly accused her of witchcraft and she was hanged.

Witnesses over the years have reported seeing a floating bright white apparition near the entrance of the mines. It is believed that she protects children from the dangers inside it. The reports of her physical features differ but the similarities have always been that she is either dazzling or bright white. This is how she got the name "White Witch."

The second "White Witch" is said to occupy the Rose Hill Cemetery located on top of a small hill just west of the main entrance to the Black Diamond Park preserve. It is reported to be the ghost of Sarah

"Granny" Norton. Sarah was a well-respected midwife who died tragically when the carriage she was riding in turned over and crushed her while on her way to deliver a baby in the town of Clayton. On the fateful day of her demise, there was a baby preparing to be born and there was no horse and buggy available to pick up Sarah from Nortonville to make the delivery. All the local buggies including all the rental buggies were at a funeral in Martinez, CA. The owner of the livery was also attending the funeral himself, leaving a stable hand in charge of the building and the daily operations of the business. When the stable hand was approached and asked for a buggy to pick up Granny Norton and bring her back to town, this inexperienced helper only had two horses in the stable remaining. The young man went to hitch up the two horses to the last remaining buggy in the shop. One of the horses had never being hooked to a buggy before and was way too skittish to be put in this stressful situation. There was a great deal of bucking and kicking during the harnessing and hitching process, but the horses were eventually lead out to the front of the stables and offered to the driver.

The buggy was then dispatched to pick up Sarah who was about four miles away and just over the hill top. Upon arriving, the driver of the buggy handed over the control of the buggy. He was reported to have made a comment that this was not an easy group of horses to handle, but it was all there was available. As she took charge of the buggy and headed back towards Clayton to help deliver the child, the inexperienced horse got spooked as it thundered down the hillside towards Clayton. The buggy flipped and Sarah Norton was tossed from the vehicle as the buggy crashed off the road and into a ditch causing the wagon to be totally destroyed. A newspaper later reported that poor Granny Norton experienced multiple compound fractures from the violent impact. Her bones were protruding through her skin as she bled out and died at the scene. The community was devastated as Sarah Norton was highly respected and loved by all in this mining community.

The stable owner and stable hand were later convicted of manslaughter, as this was not a safe thing to put a rookie horse together with another horse that had never traveled together.

Sarah Norton wasn't known to be a spiritual person and even rejected ceremony when she was asked prior to her death about her funeral arrangements. Her children tried to obey her wishes for no funeral, but the town's people decided otherwise. Since she was greatly admired, the entire town of Somersville tried twice to give her a public funeral, but failed when unnaturally fierce storms struck the area, washing out any attempts to get the body to the top of the steep hill for burial. A third attempt was made, and on this day another fierce storm hit town, but the determined townsfolk decided to suffer through the storm and hold the ceremony as planned. And so Sarah Norton was publicly laid to rest within the gates of Rose Hill Cemetery - against her wishes.

This Protestant cemetery, located on this prime piece of real estate with a glorious view, became the final resting place of mostly Welsh people who died from around 1865, up until a little after the mines closed, in 1954.

Since that day, people have reported seeing a white apparition floating between the headstones scattered throughout the cemetery. Sarah Norton hopelessly wanders the cemetery looking for a way to leave. Thus, she shares the nickname "White Witch" with the mines other ghost, Mary.

The Contra Costa Historical Society does have on record an obituary for one Sarah Norton. The date of death is listed as October 11, 1879 with no cause of death provided.

14 – Jet Fighter Sandwich

This report was submitted to National UFO Reporting Center in 2003 regarding a sighting in the Clayton area. The title of the document reads *"One orb, followed by a jet, followed, in turn, by another orb. I am not certain exactly when this happened."*

The report reads, *"I was taking an evening walk in a rural area outside the city when I saw what I first thought was a fast moving artificial satellite (although it seemed a bit low for a satellite). Then I heard a jet. I looked and saw a fighter jet come over the hilly horizon.*

It was following the light in the sky (going the exact same direction as the orb of light). Then I realized that the orb of light really was quite low and small (it could not have been larger than a VW beetle based on the size of the jet following it). Both jet and orb disappeared over the hilly horizon. I wondered "did I just see an ET craft?" Then I thought to myself "insufficient evidence for that conclusion" and a couple seconds later, another identical looking light moved through the sky in exactly the same direction as the first. There was no jet following the second light."

No other details have been released on this case even though it should be available sometime soon, when the statute of limitation expires. An investigation was made but there was never an official explanation on what had happened.

There was only the one report of the chase in the heavens over the City of Clayton. Conspiracy theorists say this was a battle for the skies between our air force and alien craft. Others say this was a covert UFO training mission. All we can do is document and leave it to the readers to decide happened that night.

15 - Mt. Diablo Folklore

As early as 1806, General Mariano Guadalupe Vallejo reported an encounter with a flying, spectral apparition, while engaged in military operations against the *Bolgones* band of the Bay Miwok Native American tribe. There was fear from his army as this disc shaped object hovered over the summit of the mountain. Could this have been an Omen or a warning to the invading Spanish forces?

The conventional view is that Mount Diablo derives its name from the 1805 escape of several Chupcan Native Americans from the Spanish into a nearby willow thicket. The natives seemed to disappear into thin air, and the Spanish soldiers thus gave the area the name "Monte del Diablo," meaning "thicket of the devil." Monte was later misinterpreted by English speakers as mount or mountain.

General Mariano G. Vallejo, in an 1850 report to the California State legislature, gave this much romanticized story of the derivation of the name of Mount Diablo from its Spanish to English form, related to the mountain and an evil spirit.

This name was later applied to Salvio Pacheco's Rancho Monte del Diablo, the present-day site of the city of Concord. The name's origin was misinterpreted by English-speaking newcomers to refer to the mountain rather than the settlement.

The name Monte del Diablo ('Mount of the

Devil') appears on the "Plano topográfico de la Misión de San José" about 1824, where there was a Native American settlement at the approximate site of the present town of Concord {Pacheco}. On August 24, 1828, the name was applied to the Monte del Diablo land grant for which Salvio Pacheco had petitioned in 1827. One attribute that makes the name Mount Diablo appropriate is that the mountain glows red at sunset due to the high amount of iron in the soil and rock.

Another account was printed in 1947 by Dorothy H. Huggins in the Western Folklore magazine starts with the heading "Legends of Mt. Diablo." It goes on to read:

James Townsend Jr., listed a few legends from the mountain.

First, there is a story from 1917 in an article from the History of Contra Costa County. The book goes on to say that when a group of local pioneers and trappers, a group was dispatched to hunt down a group of horse thieves from one of the native tribes. The natives were spotted and chased up the steep embankments of the mountainside. The natives managed to find a divide in the rocks, and with the trappers hot on their tails, they made their way into the opening. The trappers slowly moved toward the small crack in the rocks. To their horror, as they got closer, the roar of a monster came screaming out from behind the rocks and a burst of intense flame followed. With many of the trappers fearing for their lives and with many "Cararjos," turn tailed and headed quickly back down the mountain. Upon returning to their ranches and camps, the men explained that the Devil himself with the aid of his chief steward had made their home on the mountain. These never men returned to the mountain ever again.

Another account took place when the Spanish were making their way to the base of the mountain and preparing to challenge the natives around the now modern location of the city of Clayton. As the troops approached the base of the mountain, many of the soldiers witnessed what they described as dancing lights and the effigy of a man floating in the air. This was enough to abort the mission and the troops turned and headed quickly in the direction of present day Martinez, also never to return.

Yet another tale comes from the invasion of the Spanish into this somewhat peaceful area. The legend goes that there were two feuding Native American factions that lived on Mt. Diablo and could not seem to get along. One group would steal horses, then a day or so later, the other group would steal livestock. So on and so forth, back and forth for many years, until one day, the two tribes met at a secret spot at the top of the mountain.

Legend has it that the area was bathed in light and both parties agreed to end the feud once and for all with a battle at the base of the mountain. The next day both battling parties met at the base of the mountain and a battle commenced. There was bloodshed for hours and the two tribes started to dwindle in size, but as sunset approached, the two sides did not back down from the fight and continued the slaughter. On the mountain ridge, the devil himself was rooting for both sides to obliterate each other. As night fell, the glow of the devil continued to shine on the peak. Both sides were said to be under mind-control from the devil, and they completely destroyed each other. Once the last Indian breathed his last breath, the Devil; wearing his flaming garments' laughed and sang songs of joy as he gazed on the carnage that lay below.

16- Diablo's Mountain Lion

Gary Bogue was the curator of the Lindsay Wildlife Museum in Walnut Creek, California for over twelve years and he was writing a daily column about pets and wildlife for the Contra Costa Times for over forty two years before retiring in 2012.

Over the years, there have been reports of Mt. Diablo sightings of alleged "black mountain lions." Bogue felt there might have been something to these reports. He even started collecting accounts of a black panther-type cat seen putting a kill in a tree, way back in the 1970's. Bogue theorized that perhaps a thick coated leopard was around, and responsible for some of the sightings. Bogue's writings can be found online and what follows are excerpts of his writings.

One example was a mystery cat seen by Lynn

Reed and his wife Kathleen. It was first viewed at about 6:30 p.m. They said the cat was about 5 feet long and about 2 feet tall. Its head was "the size of cantaloupe" and Reed estimated it to weigh about 60 pounds.

"It was black," Reed said. "It had no other markings." One of Bogue's other readers wrote in saying the following...

"I was interested to read the story Aug. 13 about the sighting of what appeared to be a large black cat in the East Bay hills.

My husband often walks our dog in the hills of Black Diamond Regional Park. About a month ago, he told me that he had seen a large black animal at a distance, making its way down a hill across from the trail he was following. It was only in sight for a few minutes, and our dog didn't seem to see or smell it. His first reaction was that it looked like a bear, but of course he knew that couldn't be right. When he told me about it, I suggested that it might have been a wild boar, although we were not aware of boars frequenting the Black Diamond area....Cathy in Antioch."

Columnist Gary Bogue responded:

"Whenever you're out hiking in local open spaces and you see a large dark animal in the distance that looks like a bear, it's probably a wild pig.
A lot of wild pigs are on Mount Diablo and it wouldn't surprise me a bit if one strayed into the Black Diamond Regional Park area." Source: Gary Bogue, August 18, 2009.

Yes, mountain lions exist there, but *black* mountain lions are not verified zoologically. Black leopards and black jaguars are known, but they do not naturally live in the Clayton/Concord/Walnut Creek California area. But California's Black Panthers are a cryptic population with a well-established legacy, for example, that inhabits several pages of reports in the book, *Mysterious America*.

Outstanding outdoors reporter Tom Stienstra of the *San Francisco Chronicle*, known for his articles on Bigfoot, has tackled the issue of a new wave of Black Panther encounters in the Bay Area. As he notes, the *"sudden rash of 'black panther sightings' at Bay Area parks has given new spark to the region's greatest wildlife mystery."*

Despite rumors of released exotic cats, of out-of-place jaguars, or of misidentified black domestic cats, the sightings of large, black felines have a long history and continue as a mystery in several Northern California wild sites. *Mysterious America* reads the flap of sightings beginning in 1972 of the pumas seen on Mt. Diablo and the "Black Mountain Lion of Devil's Hole" often seen in Las Trampas Regional Park near San Ramon, CA, on the other side of the mountain.

Ten years of rumors of "escaped exotic beasts," caused an outbreak of panic throughout the hiking community and local residents surrounding the mountain itself. The Mt. Diablo and Bay Area Black Panthers have been actively observed for over four decades. One of the first reports of a giant cat sighting was from Marin County for September, 1964. Stienstra shares some of the recent eyewitness accounts in a section of his writings he called, *"Seeing is believing."*

Once fooled, twice right: *"People seem to think I'm 'crazy' when I told them today, that I've seen this big black cat that was not a housecat: approximately four*

~ 80 ~

feet long or so without the tail, jet black, very beautiful and sleek. I have this big ridge, part of Miller-Knox Park, right in front of my house. Every morning I hike it up to Point Richmond and walk back on the middle-level ridge trails. The first time I saw it I only got a glimpse of it from the side. I saw something black run past me. When I turned my head I just saw the back. I immediately had the thought 'mountain lion' and then immediately thought 'Nah, they don't have mountain lions here' and 'mountain lions are brown.' I thought that it's maybe a dog or maybe a deer that looked very dark. I talked myself into thinking that it must have been some kind of black deer. This morning around 8.30 a.m. or so, when I was walking in a little canyon I saw it again. No questions, a big black cat, no house cat, but a large cat. Jet black, no other colors." – Michaela Graham, Richmond.

Like a jaguar in the jungle: *"I was curious about EBMUD's protected watershed off Redwood Road in Castro Valley, so I obtained a permit and checked it out . . . I decided to navigate into the gully, walked maybe 30 or 40 feet to the east and suddenly found myself locked eyes with this big black cat. It was roughly 50 feet from me, through several barriers of logs and overgrowth. The first thought is that it looked like a panther, but the weird thing is that sort of animal should be in Africa, not the East Bay. It was so out of place".* – Larz Sherer, Berkeley.

Legend has it, one of these mountain lions was once captured, shot and carried down from the mountain and displayed in the main street of Clayton. The cat was dragged around the town and taken to every saloon in the area for people to marvel at this very rare catch. There is very little to support this lore but as many times before, it makes for a great slice of Clayton folklore.

17 -Bully Ingram

Bully Ingram is one of the more well-known folklore stories to come out of the sleepy town of Clayton. The story has been passed down through generations and is often told over dinner or at the bar. I first heard the story while drinking a beer at the Clayton Club and then subsequently it was relayed to me by the staff at the Historical Society.

There was a small, hillside cave that would now face the main street of Clayton. It was naturally formed in the steep hillside at the base of the Mitchell Creek. Atop the hill now stands the Clayton Elementary school. Back in 1826, Jedediah Strong Smith, the famous mountain man and explorer arrived in the Clayton area. Wanting to secure a drink for his steed, he made his way down the rather steep embankment to the creek that flowed below. As he approached the water, a large muscular man with dark complexion leaped from the cave and confronted Smith. The description offered by Smith after their confrontation said the cave dweller wore what appeared to be British sea faring garments. He stood over six feet tall in his knee length navel boots; he carried two dueling pistols, a dagger and a gleaming cutlass that was styled after the weaponry of navel men. With his red bandana and golden earring, he could have been a pirate of years gone by. The lore states he also wore a bone through his nose, which I personally find it hard to believe.

This strange, out of place character went by the

name Billy Ingram or Bully Ingram and he lived out his days near the Bay Miwok native Indian village. Billy was known to be an accomplished guide and knew the area very well. So when in 1836, he was approached to lead a party of the Governor of California, Michel Torena, through the area, he jumped at this opportunity to show off his skills. The party was seen closing in on the area around Clayton, Ingram met up with them in his finest outfit and with all his weapons polished and in fine working order. Ingram confided in the leaders of the party that the trip was not for the faint of heart and there were natives that might take down the party of the new Governor.

The party rested in the Clayton area and started out the following day with restocked supplies and plenty of water to carry them to their next resting point. The trek took the party into what was called Dark Canyon, which was a prime spot for native ambushes. The sides of the path were steep and the area was covered in foliage, hiding anyone that may lay in wait. Very little sunlight made it through the denseness of the trees and the ground remained damp under foot. The event was not well documented, but apparently, the group was ambushed by a group of natives that swarmed down from overhead and managed to kill a few members of the traveling party. One of those deaths was that of Billy Ingram.

It has been reported, that once in a while, in the middle of the night, a man is seen sitting on the bank, close to where the cave is believed to be. Is this a traveler just passing through the area that decided to rest for the night at this spot, or could it be the ghost of Billy Ingram waiting for another party of travelers to ask for his help?

There is a story stating this Billy Ingram was a real person and there was a cave in the hillside. A few years ago, there was a request made by the elementary school for some rubble and rocks from the quarry to fill in a sagging part of the schools playground. The area was sinking rapidly and this was a danger to the children and staff of the school. An agreement was reached and a large load of gravel was delivered and the sinking ground was then pressed down until it gave way. The hole was then filled with gravel and the black top replaced. It would have been great to take a look in the hole before it was filled in. Who knows what could have been in there. But now we are left with this lore and there no longer is a cave.

18 - Local Reports of UFO Sightings

Just like in any location throughout the country, reports have increased dramatically since the first newspaper reports of a crashed item in Roswell, New Mexico. This trend of reports have continued to this day and include reports of saucer shapes, triangular objects, and colored lights seen buzzing the skies. Listed below are documented reports and a few hand written accounts of UFO activity over the summit of Mt. Diablo. Most reports have been collected or submitted to MUFON (Mutual UFO Network), the world's leading collector of daily UFO activity throughout the world. Others have been submitted to local newspapers and have been passed down through word of mouth.

Sometimes people's accounts of the sightings are very limited and offer very little information on the incident. The following dates are accurate but the last names have been removed.

On 11/28/2003, A local from the Clayton area and seven of her friends and family saw a dull, gray triangular shaped object hover over a hill on the north east side of Mt. Diablo. It was stated that the triangular shaped object was seen flying toward the group and within a blink of an eye, the object abruptly stopped and then sped away in a different direction. There was a very quiet high pitched hum that was heard from the craft as it moved away at great speed. It also appeared to be emitting a strange kind of bluish grey haze from all sides of the craft. This sighting lasted between two and three minutes from the first sight of the object until it vanished out of sight. This report was supported by a few other people not related to this group of people. An investigation report was sent to MUFON, but the object remains unidentified.

The next reported incident occurred on 10/7/2003 when an oval/disk shaped object with a brilliant white aura moved slowly across the sky. It then stopped and then disappeared to the amazement of bystanders that were lucky enough to glance up into the heavens at that moment.

One individual wrote a report that said she saw an object in the sky that was not behaving like a normal aircraft. It was moving very slowly, and appeared to stop for brief periods of time, hovering around the summit of Mt. Diablo. It was an Oval/disk shape and had an aura of bright white light around it that occasionally shot off short beams of white light, as if it was a police helicopter with a laser beam. It was a clear day; the sky was blue, with no other aircraft or clouds to obstruct the view from the ground. The object seemed to appear, disappear, then reappear; it became dark, and then a brilliant light and aura appeared. It took the witness several minutes to figure out what was going on. When she realized what was happening she ran and got her camera out of her car that was parked nearby. It was a brand new camera and didn't have the SD memory card installed! So, the lady went back to her car, and rummaged through the packaging to find the card, the whole time she knew that the opportunity for her to take pictures of the object was wasting away.

Once the card was installed and the camera was turned on once more, the probability of the object still being visible was minuscule. The whole process was reported to take more than seven minutes. To the amazement of the female, the object was still in sight. She quickly lifted the camera and peered through the viewfinder, scanning the sky for the strange object that made no noise at all. Once she located the object in the viewfinder, she began to click away. The object was further away and headed toward the West side of the mountain near Walnut Creek. There was a moment that it appeared that her eyes were playing tricks on her as the object went through a cycle of disappearing and re-appearing. She managed to get four consecutive photos, and sometimes when it reappeared it seemed closer and then further away, as if it was either jumping around or increasing and decreasing in size. The woman often sat on her deck during the warmer months and saw a lot of aircraft, blimps, etc., flying overhead, but this object was very unusual and worthy of documentation. The report was followed with a personal request that said "I hope the photos are good enough to be magnified and analyzed, allowing identification of this object." But like so many other UFO sightings, the photos came up missing and I could not find any more details on the outcome for this fifteen minute encounter.

The next documented report was a quick one. On 9/4/2003 at approximately 8:20 PM a witness reported a circular object was seen streaking towards Mt. Diablo State Park area. A male had submitted this account on the internet, for a request to follow up from the likes of MUFON. The statement reads: "My wife and I had just returned from a local trip when we noticed something moving in the Eastern sky. We immediately saw a bright circular object moving at a high rate of speed from the sky towards the ground (best guess is that the object was two to three miles away, headed towards the Mt. Diablo State Park area at a forty five degree angle). Object appeared as a very bright green circle of light surrounding a relatively dim red light, made no sound, and disappeared after only five seconds."

The NUFORC (The "National UFO Reporting Center") has released the basic details of the following sightings. For the protection of the people submitting the stories, only the details provided on released documents are reported; the center only provided details that were from stories provided on the internet.

This is one of those stories: "Five amber lights spanning 75 yards came silently towards me from the Northeast. The lights appeared connected. Five yellow amber lights spanning 75 yards appeared as if on a large arched winged craft flying silently from the Northeast. The night was dark and clear. No craft was visible. Centered directly under the five amber lights was one white light which was meekly strobing. It appeared about 2000 feet and moved about 50 mph. When 1/2 mile away, it slowly turned 180 degrees and flew back into the direction it came from. The five lights come closer together as a group, and then independently blinked out. The craft was never seen again in this area but there was several reports of the same light formation lights the Burbank area during January and February, 2003."

19-The School Visitor

During the spring of 1983 on a warm afternoon, Mr. Taylor was showing a slide show to students in an afterschool program at the elementary school in Clayton. The slide show was ending and most of the kids had been picked up by their parents and had departed for the day. Only the teacher, a sixth grader, and a fourth grader were left in the darkened classroom with just the brightness of the projector lighting up the wall and surroundings. Behind the students was a class partition that separated two halves of one larger room. This partition was open about a foot or so, just enough to let light in from the other half of the room. As the presentation continued, Mr. Taylor was interrupted by one of the students that said out loud "That gives me shivers up and down my back." As Mr. Taylor turned to see why he was being interrupted, he noticed the child staring over his left shoulder and towards the class divider. There now stood what was described as a well over six foot tall shadow man blocking out the light through the partition. There were no facial features, just a dense darkness. It looked like a man cloaked in a faint gray hue and it did not move at all. It just stared into the room. The projector started to malfunction and jam on itself. Instinctively, Mr. Taylor turned to shut it off to prevent it from burning out and breaking. When he hit the off button and looked back to where the shadow man had been standing, it was no longer there. Whatever was there had vanished into thin air. There was no sound of footsteps walking away and no evidence of any trickery. The lights were turned on in the class room and Mr. Taylor peeked through the divider to see both the doors were closed and no one was in the room. This school was also the location of the Billy Ingram story and there have been other sightings of figures outside the building itself.

20 - Keller House Barns

The Keller Mansion was a house built in the early 1920's and was one of California's oldest cattle ranches, active into the 1970's the house was built on an old Indian grave site and native village. The barns themselves were not original to the location, but have been collected up over the years and placed next to the Keller Mansion. The original barn that stood close to this site was closer to the main road and was a huge construction that was easily seen from a distance. This barn was removed to make way for the new library that was planned for the town.

Over time the barns have become the targets of vandalism and slowly but surely the barns disappeared piece by piece as the panels came up missing. While on a trip to photograph the barns for a postcard I created for the City of Clayton and the Historical Society, a worker from the golf course called out to me and wanted to know why I was taking photos. I explained that I was writing a book and wanted photos to document my writings. He of course mentioned the mansion that stood right behind me, but I was surprised to hear a story of a shadow man that has been seen by members of the golf club staff and as well as a golfer over the past few years.

When I asked for more details, I was told that the story had come to him via word of mouth from a former employee, who heard it from someone else. The perfect folklore set up.

The story goes that during the long hot summer nights, just after the golf club has closed for the night, when the sun sets behind the mountain, the staff will do a walk through to make sure the golf course is clear. On a few occasions, when the staff made their way past the old mansion, they glanced across to the barns and something caught their attention. One staff member took off running when he saw a faceless shadow person just inside the doorway of one of the old barns. The shadow man appeared to be staring, looking at something that was not there. As the story was passed around, a golfer had stated he had seen the same image in the same location.

There is no written record of this happening, but there is word of mouth. On asking for more detail, all I got was that it was like a shadow that was cast on the ground during a sunny day, but it was three dimensional and stood vertically. Could it be the spirit of a rancher that worked in the barns and is upset that they were moved? Is it yet another report of Native American activity in the area? On inspection of the barns, it was clear that one of them was once a residence as there are remnants of wallpaper still clinging to the inside corners of the walls. The story appears to be very limited as no one else in the town seems to know of it except a few people at the golf course.

UPDATE - These barns were dismantled on the week of May 16th 2016.

21- Moresi's Chophouse

The former La Croquet Restaurant, now Moresi's Chophouse, is housed in what were once two different buildings that were built in 1857, and is the centerpiece of a local legend that started in the 1800's. Rowdy miners were said to have gotten into a shootout in the eucalyptus grove across the street from this building. This confrontation ended in a flurry of gunfire with bullets ripping through the branches and the trees. Both parties in the confrontation missed their targets and bullets found their way scattering all over the grove and a few stray shots worked their way through all the trees in the grove and out onto the main street. One of the bullets entered a window of a family residence, hitting a little girl who was playing quietly in the front room of the family home. She slumped to the floor and lay in a pool of her own blood. To the extreme horror of her parents, who tried to revive the young girl, but it was too late. Medics were called, but the poor child had bled out and passed away in the middle of her home.

When the most recent owner of the building, Ed

Moresi purchased the property, he noticed there was a blood stain close to the bar. He hired staff to try and remove the stain, but every time the hard wood area was cleaned and bleached, a few days later the blood stain would return. After many attempts at removing it, Ed decided to just carpet over the area. I was told that they can guarantee that if the carpet is lifted, that blood stain would be as prominent as any time in the past.

This is not the end of the paranormal activity within the restaurant as there is more. One occurrence happened a few hours before the steak house was ready to open for business and only the owner and a few back room employees were in the building. Ed was setting up the tables with laundered crisp white table clothes and sparkling clean wine glasses. He placed a cup of water on one of the tables and continued his tasks to prepare for opening. Then without any warning, Ed's eyes were drawn to something that was unexplainable. He witnessed the glass of water that had moved across the table and position itself on the other corner of the table. There was no rational explanation for this occurrence and remains unexplained to this day.

Many times, the light switches have been flicked in the downward position and the lights turned on, only to have the same lights turned off and the switch returned to its upright position.

It is well known by staff members that the spigot in the kitchen area will turn on all by itself and flow and then without warning, will turn itself off, leaving the sinks filled with water. Staff members have stood back in shock when they witness this happening.

So, while I was waiting to interview Ed at his Mudville Grill location in the downtown area across from the Grove, I was joined at the bar by a gentleman that introduced himself as Peter Matheson, the owner of Performance Trailer Services; a local horse trailer repair company, and also the last remaining descendent of the original pioneer Matheson family. He was on the team that renovated the now modern looking chophouse from its former condition before the building was purchased.

During the long hours of renovation, in which Matheson would work up to sixteen hours at one time, he experienced what he considered to be the spirit of Molly, a seven year old girl.

There was never any paranormal activity during daylight hours but once the sun set things would kick off. Being a skilled laborer, Peter understood the importance of tying the extension cord so it did not come apart while using a power tool. On many occasions, Peter would be drilling and the power would go out. When he investigated he saw that the knot in the cord had been undone and the two cords were separated.

While working on the project, the workers would often have the radio playing and folks would be singing along as they worked. If the radio was playing after dark, they felt the ghost of Molly did not approve of the workers off key singing, and she would turn the radio off or change the station. Sometimes she turned the radio on and let it play for a while before turning it off once more.

The same sort of activity happened with the lighting fixtures. The wiring was all brand new and everything, but the light switch incident that happened to Ed would happen to Peter and other contractors too. There was nothing worse than drilling holes and then all of a sudden being plunged into darkness. A call out to stop messing around would often return the lights to an on position.

Another example that was witnessed a few times during reconstruction was different and a lot scarier than any of the other incidents. All the other cases in this building were electrical in nature but very late one night when Peter was working in the building, he had a feeling he was being watched. He knew he was the only one there and all doors were locked and blinds were closed. As he rose to his feet and turned toward an internal doorway he witnessed what was described as a black silhouette of a Western style little girl stood in the doorway. She was semitransparent with just a small amount of light showing through her very dark vertical shadow. She did not move, she just stood there blocking the doorway. Within the blink of an eye, she was gone. This was not enough to scare off the contractor, but it was enough to halt proceedings for a time while he took a seat and try to figure out what he had just witnessed.

It was not the last time this apparition was seen. She has showed up in many spots of the old house through the years. She manifests as a dark shadow person with a small amount of light seeping through. She gives off the feeling of being a happy spirit and seems to be there to have fun with whomever she encounters. To this day, she makes appearances once in a while, and if staff sees her, they are not scared, but greet her with a "Hello Molly" and then she disappears.

If you stop in a for a meal and a glass of wine, you may be lucky to catch a glimpse of Molly as she stands in the doorway of this historical location. If you are able to see Molly, please be nice to her and say "Hi", the staff appreciates that. In her honor, the owners planted a tree in the front flower beds of the restaurant. Just as a reminder of a young innocent life that was cut short for no reason at all. Bless her soul.

22 - The Reporter's Stay

There are handwritten notes in the files of the Clayton Historical Society that have not been seen in many years. One of these notes was found on a scrap piece of lined paper and hand written in blue ink. The paper was dated February 1st 1997 in the top right hand corner, and is now faded with age.

The first line starts out by saying "*I have found this article in some old newspapers I had collected and I thought you would find it a lot of fun and interesting.*" The letter was signed by Mrs. E. Esser and hand delivered to the museum by her husband, Fortyhe. The letter goes on to say that the family that included younger children decided to attend an alleged haunted location in the Town of Clayton. This was part of a tour put together by long time historian and ghost walk host Richard Taylor. The family was told stories that rotated around the two-story home that was looking a little worse for wear by the late 1990's. The small group entered the location and positioned themselves throughout the living room. With the lights turned off, all the windows firmly locked and all doors closed, the group went quiet as they listened for any form of paranormal activity. Then, out of the blue, there was a chilling pillar of ice cold air that moved throughout the group. One by one each person felt the cold pass them. The cold spot did not just move in one direction, like a wind or draft, but seemed to move in a straight line then move to the people on the left side of the room and return to its starting position. It was enough to startle the letter writer and caused them to submit their experience. The letter referred to a close friend of the Esser family who worked for the local newspaper as a reporter and did not believe in ghosts or spirits and thought the whole idea was contrived and ridiculous to say the least.

The reporter, whose name is not known, asked permission to return to the location and spend the night to debunk all the crazy claims that were circulating. The reporter was given permission and found himself on the doorstep with a thermos of soup and a sleeping bag. After being offered access to the home, the homeowner told him the unusual stories and wished him a peaceful night's sleep. The home owner closed the door behind him and the lock clicked into the locked position. The reporter poured a cup of soup and settled in for the night. He lay on the old couch waiting for something to happen. He relaxed with his drink and a note pad and pen at the ready to document any activity that occurred.

The evening transitioned into night time and only the street lights shined through the windows. It was noted there was no movement of the curtains throughout the house, which would mean the windows were tightly sealed or there was no wind at all. The note goes on to say that after a few hours of nothing but passing traffic noise and the occasional pedestrian, things started to happen around the house. The reporter stated that the house started to feel as if it was sinking in water as the air was hard to breathe. Everything around him started to appear a lot darker than before, even though the sun had set many hours before. The reporter was startled by the sound of slamming doors in the garage. He got up to check and see if the wind was causing the noise. The doors of the garage were wedged open and held in place by bricks. The wind could not have slammed the doors and reset them in the same locked position. Being a skeptic, the reporter returned to his sleeping bag and put the action down to wind but moments later, the same thing happened once again.

This time the reporter did not hesitate to jump up and try and catch the person he assumed was making all the noise to scare him. He flung open the door to the garage and the second he peeked out though the open door the banging and crashing stopped. Everything was thrown into total silence once more. This was becoming a concern to the reporter as he returned to his sleeping bag for a second time and picked up his note pad to write the account of what had just happened. Hours passed and the reporter drifted into a deep sleep. It appeared that the activity of the night had ended and that the rumors of this place being very haunted were put down to wind or a prank played by a couple of local kids.

The reporter was awoken in the early hours of the morning by what sounded like the homeowner climbing the stairs. The skeptic jumped to his feet and called out to whoever was walking up the stairs. The footsteps continued without any hesitation to respond to the reporter's request to identify whom was making them. It was as if whoever it was, could not hear him calling out to them. What was very unnerving to the reporter was the footsteps stopped at the top of the stairs and went no further. This meant there must be a person standing at the top of the stairs looking down on him. He walked in a very deliberate way so to hear any movement on the stairs and popped his head around the corner and looked upward. To his total horror, there was no one there. He had; without any doubt, heard what sounded like weighted boots climbing the staircase, the clunking of the heels on the bare wooden steps and the sound of the creaking of the wood under the weight of the person. To add to his dismay, the reporter noticed the stairs were covered in carpet which would have made the hard wood clunking sound impossible. Now the reporter had the fear of God in his soul, but being a skeptic he set out to prove there was someone in the building.

He slowly made his way up the stairs and

noticed not a sound was heard from his feet hitting each step as the carpet muffled any impact of his boots. Once at the top of the stairs, the reporter called out and received nothing in response. He flicked on the hallway light, then, gingerly walked from room to room looking for whoever entered the building. He found no one in the house and all windows were locked shut. He sat down on one of the beds and tried to make scene of what had just happened.

Then once more he heard the same heavy boots clunking up the stairs, but this time it was coming toward him and not away from him. With no means of protection if this was a home invasion, he mustered up all his strength and waited at the top of the stairs for whoever was ascending. The footsteps got louder and louder, the closer the person got to the top of the stairs, then there was silence once more. He jumped forward to see who was standing on the stairs and as he stood in the doorway and glanced down the lit hallway, there was no one there. In a state of fear, he took off down the stairs at a frantic rate, grabbed his stuff and headed out the front door. His days of being a skeptic were surely over and his experience proved to him that there is more to life after death.

The reporter was never named but other people involved with this story requested to not be named for fear of ridicule or just the fear of stirring something up from the past. The letter itself ends with a cheerful story of Mrs. Esser driving school buses through the old town and how much she had missed her job since retiring.

23 - Contra Costa County Big Foot Report

Even the Clayton /Mt. Diablo region is not out of reach of Bigfoot accounts. This one really is a stretch but it was reported and so it can go down as folklore. The report was submitted to BFRO (Bigfoot Field Researchers Organization) in February of 2000. The location is described as the base of the Diablo Foothills, in the East Bay in California. The report number is 166 and falls under the distinction of (Class B). The reporter said that two people experienced the incident. They were both awoken around 2:00-3:00AM, by a very unnatural howling sound. It sounded as if a pack of wild dogs was running past the house. They didn't hear any footsteps though, just a very odd howling. It was a mixture of howling and heavy wind combined. Note, it wasn't windy that night. They heard it for about ten seconds, as it went past the house and kept going. They heard the sounds fade in the distance as it ran off. They both sat there terrified, saying "What the #$%$# was that?" They didn't go outside to check it out, rationalizing that it had to be a pack of dogs, or coyotes or something. Until reading the Bigfoot site, they hadn't really thought much more of it but this could have been one of the only reports of a Bigfoot in the area.

24 - The Back Yard Shadow Man

This story was posted on the internet, so you have to take it with a grain of salt. I have searched for other accounts of a similar experience in the area from where this report was made, but I was unable to get any confirmation from anyone.

The story reads: "I grew up in a mobile home park, and I had a strange thing happen there that I will always wonder about. I was a teenager when this occurred. I woke up from a nap in my living room and was thirsty. As I walked to the kitchen, I could hear my brother watching television. It was just after sunset, and as I approached the sink I stared out the kitchen window frozen in fear. I began screaming at the top of my lungs and could hear my brother's approach. He called my name repeatedly, but I could not move or stop screaming. My brother continued to call and shake me and finally slapped me. This brought me out of my frozen state, and to this day I wonder what I saw outside that window that frightened me. It appeared to be a form of a shadow person that was motionless but solid in consistency. There was no face or features, just an outline of what appeared to be a shrouded figure." Name Withheld

There have been no other recorded incidents since this one happened on Marsh Creek Rd., Clayton.

There have not been any more reports from this location.

25- Morgan Territory Rd Image

Morgan Territory Road is an old logging road that was built back in the 1800's to bring wood from Santa Cruz to the Eastern Contra Costa County. The road cut through the wilderness connecting the towns of Livermore and Clayton. It is a very isolated road, and there have been many reports of strange happenings. One of the Legends is of Joaquin Murrieta, California Bandit El Dorado; it is believed that Joaquin has buried his loot somewhere in the Morgan Territory area under an oak tree.

In the 1950's, a woman and her husband were on their way home from Livermore when they saw a spirit standing next to an oak tree off the side of the road. Not knowing the story about the loot, they just thought that they were seeing things, due to the darkness of the road

and them being tired. Once they started telling the story to their friends and family, they found out the background about the loot of Joaquin Murrieta. From time to time, people still report seeing his ghost on Morgan Territory Road, but they can never find the spot again when they go back to look for the loot that is believed to be buried there.

26- Miwok Folklore

Miwok (also spelled Miwuk, Mi-Wuk, or Me-Wuk) can refer to any one of four linguistically related groups of Native Americans, indigenous to Northern California, who traditionally spoke one of the *Miwokan* languages in the Utian family. The word *Miwok* means *people* in their native language. The group that settled in the valley between the Hills of the Black Diamond mines and Mt. Diablo were just a small group of many villages that resided throughout the area. There were between 280,000 and 340,000 Miwok that resided in the State during the mid 1700's.

The Miwok believed that Mt. Diablo was the sacred birthplace of the World. The supernatural beings known as the *"First People"* lived on the sides of the mountain. The First People were responsible for making the Indian race and supplying them with the bountiful and beautiful world that surrounded them. This included buffalo roaming the land and eagles flying through the sky. It was the perfect habitat for these hunters and gatherers that lived off the land.

The First People were also credited with sharing in-depth knowledge of natural cycles to the village chiefs and spiritual leaders. These supernatural entities were also celebrated once a year at the base of the mountain, in what would have been modern day Clayton. Neighboring groups gathered during one scheduled week to conduct what was called the "Big Times" event. This included ceremonial feasting, dancing, the trading of goods and social bonding. Most of the time there was social balance during the event but if there was a feud, the issue was brought to the forefront and with the help of the spirits they solved their differences.

There is a warning that sometimes 'when passing Too'-cha-mo the stump you hear a noise inside; it is Soo-lek'-ko the Ghost. You had better go right on, for if you stop he might do you harm. Whenever you see Poo'-ki-yu the Whirlwind whirling the dust around and around and carrying it up into the air you may know that Soo-lek'-ko the Ghost is inside, dancing and swinging round and round. You had better not go near it but keep away.'

Most Native Americans believed in the spirits of the dead. Although a person may have been a good friend while alive, if their spirit came back after death it was regarded as bad luck. Ghosts revisited the earth every night. They appeared to friends and relatives in dreams, begging them to join them in the after world. Ghosts would curse family and friends and try to make them kill others and take them to the spirit world.

Because of the danger of ghosts, most people were buried far away from their home villages. That way the spirits of the dead could not cross the river to return to their former villages. The spirits of the mountain are said to still haunt the valley and the mountain itself. Many times the images of Native Americans are seen throughout the Clayton neighborhoods.

One other story that was told of this area was that of the landscape of California which was totally covered in water with the exception of two land masses. One being Eagle Mountain and the other Mt. Diablo. There were no human inhabitants but there were two spirits that lived on these mountains. One was Good and the other was Evil. There was a great battle and Good won, destroying Evil.

The story states that there was only one coyote that lived on the peak of Mt. Diablo and now there was nothing left on Eagle Mountain. One day the lonely coyote saw a feather floating on the water and as it made its way to the island shoreline, it turned into a beautiful eagle with bright and majestic feathers. The coyote was so happy that he now had a friend and the two of them grew close. Once in a while the two would make excursions to other islands to explore.

The eagle would fly and the coyote would swim. It was decided that the two of them would counsel and they decided to make man and Native American Indians. With this agreement, the Indian population grew and the water recessed, leaving many Indian tribes and fertile land for farming.

27- Hand Written Account

This story was from hand written documents that were found in library records. The writing goes as follows: A picture was taken of a certain tree in the Black Diamond Mines area reputed to have developed ghostly images of disembodied heads hanging from its branches. The whereabouts of the photograph are unknown

The report starts with: *"First, my dad's account (this occurred in the late 60's or early 70's and is my best recollection of what he told the family): I was driving home from work and I had taken the shortcut from Kirker pass (near Clayton) to Antioch via the back roads near the Black Diamond Mines and Nortonville (this was in the days when that roadway was still open to the public). I had gotten most of the way through when I experienced car trouble. I managed to get the car to the side of the road and parked it. I then began walking along the road leading toward Antioch. This stretch of road is not well traveled, and I had little hope of getting a ride, and as it was getting toward dusk, I was a bit concerned, not having a flashlight or other emergency supplies. Lady luck smiled upon me that evening, for I heard a vehicle on the road behind me. I turned and spotted a horse drawn wagon and a solitary driver coming toward me. He offered me a ride, and I thanked him and got in. My driver said nothing to me and I followed suit. Soon, we arrived within sight of Antioch, and I jumped down from the wagon. I looked out toward the town and then turned back to thank my rescuer, and he was nowhere to be seen! I was then gripped by a cold chill to realize that I had just been given a ride by a ghost! I never took that shortcut again, and shortly thereafter, it was closed to general public.*

In an effort to corroborate my recollection with what my Dad experienced, I emailed him and he had this to say: "Mary, I do remember, and it is true it scared the hell out of me. I'll try to get online and look at it. Miss talking to you. love you Dad."

This particular area is known for strange paranormal occurrences, and there is a spot along a lonely stretch called "gravity hill" which pulls a car uphill even though the motor is off."

28 - Keller Mansion / Ranch

The property known as the Keller Ranch is thought to have been the principal village site of the Chupcan or Volvon people who occupied the areas around Mt. Diablo dating back three to four thousand years. The land currently occupied by the Keller House may have been a part of Rancho Del Diablo, a Mexican land grant. It was subsequently owned by Joel Clayton.

Vincent Liberty was a rancher and operated a "road house" on the Fairfax-Bolinas Road. Vincent Liberty left his wife in Marin County in 1891. His twenty four year old daughter, Elodia, chose to live with him and his son remained in Marin County with his wife, Mary Jane Liberty. Vincent leased the ranch on the Clayton property and he and Elodia lived in the house. The Keller house, named Casa Del Sierra, "has been locally identified as a rare surviving building of this period and a fine example of custom home building of the early twentieth century." It is of the Mission Style with Craftsman elements. Magnificent gardens and a fish pond surrounded the home, tended by Elodia. The property had large barns and cattle yards.

Harry Keller operated the ranch until his death at the end of 1940. From 1940 until her death in 1954, Elodia Liberty Keller retained a life estate of the property but it was leased it to Bob Flackus. From the early1960's until 1972, trustees of the Keller estate leased the property to Manuel DeJesus who continued ranch operations. The building was finally moved to its present location to avoid demolition. It is now used as a storage site for the library. There were plans to renovate the location, but the funds ran dry.

Rumor has it that if you take a trip down into the basement of the Keller House, you'll find more than the furnace, but you would have found a full Native American skeleton preserved in the stone walls. This story has roots in fact as there is a written report with details of many items that were removed from the basement. A couple of the items that were discovered on the property included hand carved rock mounted in mortar; and bowls ranging in size from five and a half inches to approximately eight inches, all hollowed out. Mounted in the walls of the external structure of the home, they found unusual shaped sandstone rocks with holes drilled into them. They were clearly man-made. The researchers claimed that the rocks were found in the rose garden and in the hole where the pond was made.

As the dirt floor of the basement was excavated, there was clear evidence that this was a "Burial site." With the term "Midden Face Forms SE Walls." listed in the official university report of the dig. This translated means that there were burial items beside the skeleton

~ 122 ~

that was found under the dirt floor. "Many cup-shaped receptacles made of hard material, in which ingredients are crushed or ground into the dusty floor as well as pots used especially in cooking or pharmacy were also found throughout the basement dig site". as also reported in the final documents on the dig.

Circular boulders were found outside that showed Petroglyphs in the shape of people and even modern day chess pieces. These rocks were pulled from the stream that ran past the homestead and decorated the entrance way to the ranch.

When it comes to paranormal activity, the stories are very vague. One account was that a mischievous spirit moved items around within the house. Items would be laid on a table, and minutes later the items would be gone, only to be found in the strangest of locations.

I found a person who used to spend her evenings visiting the children in the Keller House. This person wanted to remain anonymous but did describe an occurrence that happened around Christmas time when the house was decorated with a tree and all the trimmings. The kids were playing close to the kitchen door when they looked up to see the door latch lifting and the door knob turning as if someone was coming into the room. The kids moved away from the door so as not to get knocked over when the door swung open. The door started to swing open but to the shock of the kids, there was no one standing at the top of the steps leading into the home. The door then swung closed and the door re-latched itself. This was enough to cause the visitor to leave the house in a hurry and run home to tell her parents of the strange happening at the Keller House.

After the house was closed and the windows boarded up to prevent vandalism, the house started to crumble into disrepair. A group of laborers were asked to go into the basement of the house to do some routine maintenance work. It was not too much later that the contractors left the building vowing never to enter the house again. They had clearly experienced something in the basement that scared them half to death. I have been unable to track down these contractors to interview them but a report said they refused to speak of what happened down in the basement of the old ranch house.

On a recent trip with Jenny to document some of the Indian relics in the building, Jenny stated she felt something brush her hair while standing in what was once the main living room. She put it down to cobwebs, but this was felt at the same time a cold breeze passed her by. She also felt that uncomfortable cold spot in a few other isolated spots within the old house. She did not attribute any of the experiences to paranormal activity. Her descriptions do match the feelings others have reported when in the house. To this day we still do not know what scared off the laborers that were working in the basement of the home. From what I have been told the scariest item down there is the huge amounts of Black Widow spiders that have now made this their residence.

Note: There is no access to this location and the area is guarded by the police.

29 - Golf Course Para Mist

One of the newer stories that came out of the downtown Clayton area was a chance meeting I had with a gentleman outside of a store in the month of January of 2016. I had heard a rumor of an apparition seen near the golf course close to the Old Keller Mansion. I heard of this story from the folks in the sub shop next to the bocce ball courts.

After doing research in the Clayton Club, the bartender told me the tale of a ghost that passed through a man as he walked home one night. I put the story down to a night of drinking and thought nothing more of it. But a few weeks later, I heard the story again from another local, so I thought I would follow up on it.

The man involved in the story is a well-known person in the community and is well respected. The man found his way to the Clayton Club for a drink before walking home to his house on the other side of Clayton Road. There is a tunnel that passes under the road and opens up next to a babbling stream and a worn dirt path that winds its way North and into the subdivision and newer houses in the City of Clayton.

This man had two drinks at the bar and then decided it was time to walk home. His walk home was a short ten minutes, and with a steady pace, he made his way out into the darkness of the late evening. After crossing the street and heading across what was once the city baseball diamond on the corner of Oak Street and Main Street which is now just an open lot. The man entered the dark tunnel which went under the busy Clayton Rd. As the man exited the tunnel, he turned to his left to make the walk towards his home. As he approached Peacock Creek, the path was paved and hugged the side of the manicured golf course. The moon lit his way as he took the path that he had taken many times in the past. But this night his walk was different than any other one he had taken since moving to Clayton many years before.

As he walked the path he noticed what appeared to be a hazy white mist in front of him on the side of the pathway near the fence that separated the path and the golf course. This caused him to slow his pace and try and figure out what he was looking at. He wondered if it was a swarm of bugs or dust that had been kicked up by the wind. Thinking this was the case the man continued his walk down the paved pathway. As he got closer, it became evident that this was not dust or bugs that were confronting him. The color was a heavy white to grayish in appearance. The mist was the height of a man and stood motionless. The man stopped in his tracks as he was now within a few feet of this fog. Then out of the blue, the fog disbursed and vanished. The man could not believe his eyes but continued his walk right through the spot where the mist had been. Shrugging off what appeared to be a supernatural experience, he continued his walk towards home. He walked a few paces more and glanced over his shoulder. To his horror, the fog had reappeared in the exact same spot that it was moments before. Was the mysterious fog the spirit of a local native? Or could this have simply been a case of nature working her magic mixed with the injection of a few alcoholic beverages running through his veins?

An interesting side note to this story; I was telling my tales in the back room of the Clayton

Historical Society, when Renee Wing said she had heard a similar story and returned to her office to retrieve a business card that was pinned on the wall. She read it to confirm it was the correct card then handed it to me. Written in the corner was a note that said "Ghost on 14th Hole". I thanked her and took the card home with me. The following day while writing this book I sent an e-mail to confirm this was not the same person I was talking to outside of the store a week or so before. Continuing working a message came back stating the e-mail was undeliverable. Thinking the person may no longer work for this company, I decided to call the phone number on the card and asked if they knew the where abouts of the man named before me. There was a long pause and the front desk lady responded with "there is no one here by that name." It was apparent that this was a fake business card and a fake story. This mystery person's story was not the same as the one listed above. The fake story has a beam of light hitting the 14th hole as it rose from the ground.

The paranormal field is full of crazy people and you really need to be careful when working in this field.

Maybe people do is sort of stuff for attention or there is something deeper and more disturbing going on. I shredded the card and we all moved on.

30 -De Martini Winery / City Offices

The De Martini winery building is a fifty foot by sixty six foot, three story stone and wood structure set into a hillside just off of Clayton Road on the opposite side of the road from the downtown area. The bottom two floors of the ten-thousand square foot building are made of two-foot thick limestone from Joshua Marsh's quarry on the north side of Mt. Diablo, and the third floor, hillside level, is built of wood. The date "1885" is chiseled on three inner walls of the winery that are now hidden under drywall panels. Also, the name "P. De Martini" and a silhouette of a man's face with initials "P.D.M." next to it are carved on inner walls of the second floor. You will be out of luck if you wanted to observe these markings today, as the whole building is covered in drywall paneling and offices segregate the former spacious open floor plans.

The offices are filled with city officials and staff as well as the local police department. Getting anyone to admit there are strange things going on is very difficult as this is not the sort of location people share ghost stories. But one member on the third floor who often stays late; many times alone, has experienced a few strange occurrences and he was willing to share them with me.

He reported the elevator has a tendency to operate on its own. With all the doors locked to the building, he heard the elevator was summoned to the first floor and then it made its way to the third floor and the door opened. Normally the elevator would remain on that floor, but instead, it returned to other floors.

Another account from someone on the first floor reported someone once standing in the window looking out, motionless. The image appeared in old style clothing. The witness said that they stood outside and just stared at the figure in the window until it turned and appeared to walk back into the building and out of sight.

Cold spots have been recorded on all floors of

the building and a few people have experienced what is called "the cobweb effect." This is when it feels like you have walked through a cobweb. It has also been described as if someone was stroking their hair.

The final report states that there are often the sounds of people walking around within the building late at night. One person experienced what sounded like people working on the ground floor. While the male witness stood at the top of the stairs listening to the sounds coming from below. It was described as if there was a factory in full production, with a mixture of voices and the sound of objects being moved around. The sounds went on for a few minutes and then it slowly faded away to total silence. It was a little disturbing to the remaining person in the building, but according to him "We are here to co-exist with whatever is in the building; They don't harm me and I don't harm them. I like to keep our ghosts happy."

The building is off limits to ghost hunters and only available for City business.

31- Clayton's Own Alien Water Distribution Company

In the fall of 1997, there appeared an ad in the National Enquirer for *"Elemental Water and Crop Circle Energy."* The ad was a small two inch by two inch in size with a return address of a P.O. Box in Clayton, CA. The ad itself was nothing to write home about. It was just a plan text among other ads for X-Ray specs, original mummy bones and the ability to be a millionaire in five easy steps.

While I researched this book, I met up with an English chap from the London area. He is a well-educated individual and spent many years of his life educating others. He is now retired but still an active member of the Clayton community, and is seen every weekday in the old town area. As I sat with him one evening taking notes on local folklore, he expressed that he had a story for me, if I felt it was worthy of printing. I took a more relaxed posture in my rickety wooden chair and started to ask for details.

As we settled in, this man, we will call him Terry described that he and his family took a trip back to his homeland so his American born children could see where their father was born. During a day trip from London to Wiltshire to visit Stonehenge, a supernatural incident or practical joke had occurred. The formation of a crop circle had appeared overnight in an adjacent field. This crop circle was not like any of the others that had shown up in the fields of Wiltshire at that time. This circle was not a circle at all, but an array of large circles surrounded with small circles and in the shape of a pinwheel.

There was a cult following regarding these circles that were popping up all over the West Country of England. Paranormal groups insisted that these were landing sites for UFO's and others thought they were some sort of message from the heavens. Many people believe they are the result of a couple of brothers with advanced knowledge of geometry.

During Terry's visit, he decided he would take home a few ears of wheat that had been meticulously laid down on its side and pressed into place. He thought nothing of it and the wheat was stored away in his luggage and shipped back to the States.

When he and his family got home and unpacked their bags, this small item of curiosity was put on a shelf and forgotten. Time passed and it came to the attention of the family that there was an excess of green algae built up on the left side of their fish tank. The thickness of the deposits was much more than that of the rest of the tank. Terry decided to clean the tank and when he was preparing, he found that the wheat was resting against the side of the glass tank where the algae was growing out of control.

The fish tank was cleaned and the wheat was just taking up space. The wheat was then tossed out in the back yard and forgotten once more. Nothing happened out of the ordinary and time passed by. One day, while staring out the back window of his home, he noticed that there was a huge patch of grass that had sprouted up and was different than the other grass in the rest of the yard. It appeared as if this area of grass was heavily fertilized and watered more than any other area. Not thinking anything it, Terry pulled out the lawn mower, fired up the motor, and started mowing. When he approached the tall grass, he noticed a bag that lay within the tall twisted grass. Afraid of damaging his mower, Terry stopped the spinning blades and bent down to remove the object. Once grasping the bag he realized that this was the bag that he discarded a few weeks before that contained the ears of wheat. The wheat remained in perfect condition but the bag had seen better days. This was the same sort of reaction that the algae had had weeks before. For a second time the wheat was discarded and this time it was tossed in with the cultivated garden as an experiment to see if there was anything going on with the wheat and it's interaction with whatever it came in contact with. It had become apparent that there was some sort of reaction between the wheat and anything it contacted. Could this have been something to do with the so called supernatural incident that had happened just outside of the sacred rings of Stonehenge?

Terry is a man of great intelligence and an entrepreneur, so he saw an opportunity in harnessing the "powers" that were connected with his now beloved wheat ears.

Terry set about manufacturing and distributing the energy that built up in the wheat and sell it. First he took the wheat and placed it between four jars of pure water. After leaving it in the large container for one lunar cycle, the water was then drained into tiny glass vials and capped off from the outside air. A tiny amount of blue coloring was added to give it an azure harmony. Each small flask was then decorated and shipped out with a letter explaining it benefits. The letter stated: *Elemental Water and Crop Circle Energy,*

"We do not know the origin or purpose of crop circles but many people have come to believe they are communications from an energy source or consciousness unrecognized by our limited scientific view. People entering formations feel the presence of a positive energy field and have been subtly changed by the experience. Many have noted that simple objects – especially elementals such as water – are affected also." This was a link to the production of the water vials which were being sold. The letter continued: *"The formations frequently appear on the Earth's ley lines, and research has shown that the sites produce a more vigorous crop growth the next year."* This statement was very true as Terry had witnessed it firsthand. Then in bold letters same the line that read:

"*The individual plants of the crop are transmuted to store the energy.*"

The letter goes on to say that healers from all

over the World have recognized the fact that water retains the power of added biological medicals even after successive dilutions have removed all scientifically measurable trace it. The idea of the water vial instead of a small sample of wheat is that homeopathic transmutation of pure water, wheat gathered from crop formations irradiates or transfers its energy to water kept within its orbit.

The bottom line for purchasing a vial was stated as the following:

"*A simple vial of this water if worn or carried within the para-luminosity of one's personal aura, seems to energize creativity, bring calmness and a new sense of cosmic integration and oneness. Animals and even plants are similarly affected.*" Many folks break out a dictionary on this one, but so many people do believe in this method of energy.

The vials sold out but the manufacturer decided the expense and the effort was not worth his time and put an end to the production of this product. We never knew if it worked or if people throughout the world were helped by this incredible creation that was made as a fleeting idea. All we can say now is this was a product that was manufactured in Clayton, California and was strange enough to make it into this book of local Folklore.

32 - The Signs of a Lost Son

I recently put together a display of civil war artifacts in the Clayton Historical Society Museum. One day a woman came in and asked to speak to me regarding the display. She wanted information on Civil War era items that were in her family's possession. We got talking, and after a while the subject turned to my writing and my other books. The first book I wrote was about the paranormal and how it affected me personally. This lady we will call her "Kim," said she had a paranormal story and wanted to share it with me. I asked for basic details and then I did research as I have done for all the stories in this book. I was sent the following text from the detailed records that Kim kept and interpreted as signs from the dead. This is her very sad and personal accounts.

"September 26, 2013, Clayton.

I had a random thought about where we would all be buried. I have an older son who just married, so I knew he would be with his wife. I have a middle son, and my hope for him would be that when his time came, he'd have his own family and they would be together. But my thought was that I would be with my youngest son."

"September 27, 2013, Clayton 8:15 AM
Getting ready for work. I look up and say, "he would be better off ..," I stopped and said, "No, not really. I don't mean that." (My son had personal struggles)"

"8:40 AM I hear sirens nearby."

"8:53 AM I sent a text and said I hope all is OK.

That afternoon I got word that he had died in a car accident. It occurred at 8:22 AM.
My text was sent to my son at 8:53. He was

pronounced deceased at 8:52....."

"Feb 1, 2015, Clayton.

My son bought a wind chime as a Mother's day gift for me in 2014. I have a garden I started out back for my son that passed. The chime was for the garden.

Early on the morning of Feb 1, 2015, I noticed one of the strings on the chime had broken. I wanted to restring it with some fishing line. We don't have any at the house (my husband doesn't fish!) so I was going to buy some in the next day or so. Later that afternoon, about 3 PM, I was walking into my room and as I walked in the room, I looked down on the carpet and there was about a yards worth of fishing line just lying there!! There was absolutely no explanation for it....."

"March 17, 2015 9:30 PM, Clayton.

I was upstairs on my back deck as I usually do at night. I was talking to my son, as I do most every night. I usually say a prayer and just talk to him. I can see the cemetery from my house.

At night it is easy to spot because the chapel's light is

always shining bright. The lights are my focal point when I talk to my son. For about 3 nights they have been off and I'd been disappointed. I closed my eyes, telling my son I missed him so much and that I really liked when the lights were on, when I opened my eyes to go back inside, I looked over and the lights were on!"

"Thanksgiving, 2015 9 PM, Clayton.
I was out on the upstairs back deck talking to my son. I had recently added a string of solar lights to his garden. They looked really pretty. I said to my son, "Aren't they beautiful, I know you see them and like them too!" Instantly, the street light behind the garden went out......"

"Jan 9, 2016, 9:35 PM, Clayton.

Usual night time out on upstairs back deck talking to my son.....

I was telling him that I'd been feeling sad and thinking about him all day. I told him to please send me some "In my face signs" I asked, "Do you hear me??"

A few seconds later, the street light that was out, flashed on and then went out about a minute later........."

"Jan 10, 2016 6:30 PM, Clayton.

Leaving the memorial service of a friend that had just lost a child. I was very upset. I knew what this family was going through, plus it stirred up a lot of my emotions."

"Another street light all of a sudden went out right in front of me. I think that was from my son... he knew how upset I was."

"9:15 that night. Back deck as usual talking to my son about friend's service telling him to find her in heaven. Just then, the street light behind the garden went out."

"Feb 2, 2016, 8 PM, Feb 27, 2016, March 8, 2016, Clayton.

Same situation out on deck talking. Street lamp flicks out. Kind of a long story but just want to tell it because there is absolutely no explanation..."

"June 22, 2015, away on vacation in Idaho.

All day from the moment I woke up, I was an emotional wreck. Missing my boy so much. Lots of tears hidden from all except me and my son..

3PM – I'm sitting upstairs reading a book about Signs from the Afterlife. My husband puts a CD on to play. I had never heard this one before. It's really pretty music by Daniel Lanois. I am reading the chapter on "Songs." So I am reading with the CD playing in the background. The LAST song on the CD starts playing. It's Amazing Grace, presented like I've never heard before. It was beautiful, simply beautiful, my eyes were tearing."

"Now, I do know that this song is a traditional song used at memorial services. I had it at my son's but I chose it because I truly felt the words were specific to his life. (For example, I once was lost, but now I'm found....) I immediately jotted this coincidence down. (i.e. reading the song chapter in the sign book and this particular song came on)

Meanwhile, my husband goes out to do some errands,

and I go to the community pool for a few hours with my daughter."

"6:15 PM. She and I come back from pool. My husband is still out. My daughter is downstairs watching TV and I am upstairs making a puzzle enjoying the quiet. We had been back about 15 minutes when all of the sudden I hear music quietly playing. I thought maybe it was coming from downstairs but realize there is no music player downstairs. Then I think it must be the neighbor. (We were staying in condos) Then I realize the song playing is Daniel Lanois, Amazing Grace.... I tentatively get up and walk to our stereo cabinet. I CANNOT believe this song is playing. How?? How??? I broke down in tears. I was amazed and so happy. It was from my son. I know it!!!! There is no other explanation. I told my husband and daughter. They said the cd was probably just playing. I said, I would have heard it before then, if it were playing. There was NO music playing. It was just this song. The CD had ended about 30 minutes prior to us all leaving earlier."

33 - Face in the Mirror

This story is a short tale and originates from The Village Oak Shopping Center Ladies Bathroom just south of the old town of Clayton. A group of local beauticians from the Center's beauty shop once reported that every time they used the restroom, they felt like they were being watched. There was never any proof; just the possibility there could be some sort of perverted foul play going on, so the police department was notified. Upon closer examination, there was no sign of anything suspicious and the police went about their day, they explained that there was nothing to worry about.

Later, a police officer patrolling the area one evening noticed that the door to the ladies bathroom was open, and stopped to investigate the unusual situation. He entered the bathroom only to find the place completely empty. But as he turned around and faced the mirror, he saw the image of a Hispanic man standing over his shoulder in the corner. It was enough to make the officer spin on his heels and reach for his gun, only to find there was no one standing behind him. He glanced in the mirror once more and saw nothing but his own reflection.

According to psychics who visited the bathroom, the shopping center was built over an old creek, where a Hispanic man was brutally killed and buried, the bathroom lies directly over the murder site.

Did our friendly local police officer witness the ghost of the dead man? Was the man trying to relay a message about his death or was this a form of warning? What the women felt could well have been the presence of this ghostly apparition wandering his murder site. Since this event, the building has been left vacant and is currently available for rent.

34 - More UFO Reports

Here are the handwritten reports from a few people that believe that they have witnessed flying saucers around the Clayton area. None of these claims were ever proven as being UFO's by the government or State. *"In the summer of 1980, I came out of the grocery store with the bag boy and noticed something in the sky.*

It was approaching sunset and I could see a bright shining object in the sky. I knew it was not a star because it moved. I asked the bag boy what the object was and he was clueless as well. I drove home looking at the object, not wanting to lose track of it. I went home and asked my father, who worked as a nuclear physicist at the Lawrence Livermore Laboratories what the object was.

I figured he would know since he has put satellites up in space. He told me it was a weather balloon or a slow moving plane and went back to work in his den. About 45 minutes later, I advised my father that the object was still in the sky and that it was beginning to move around. My father turned white as a ghost and came running out to see the object."
Name withheld.

"We lived on farm land in a newly developed house. Our backyard view was a large field and Altamont Pass (mountains) with Mount Diablo in the distance. So we had a great view of what we saw. Anyhow, my entire family came outside to watch the object in the sky and then the neighbors on both sides of

~ 149 ~

our home came outside to see as well. This was around 8:00 p.m. in the evening.

The objects danced around in the sky and darted here and there. I ran into the house to get my father's binoculars. The object was triangular (almost like the letter "A") shape with lights on all three points. A few hours later the objects flew in the direction of Mount Diablo (Mount of the Devil, as the Indians called it.. a coincidence? I don't think so) and disappeared behind it or on it? That night on channel 7 (news scene S.F.) a reporter named Van Amburg presented a story about an object in the sky. It was a short uneventful segment about what people reported seeing, however, nothing was ever mentioned about it again on the news.

However, every night... I mean, every night around 1 or 2 in the morning I would wake up not knowing why. I would look out my window and it was there. It was like it knew I was there watching it. I watched it for a while and then it would fly away over Mount Diablo. This happened every night. I told my mother on occasion, but no one ever thought it was that important. I don't remember if it ever stopped or if I just forgot about it as I turned 18 years old and moved out."

Name Withheld

A verbal account that was offered to me stated that this lady had just finished her evening/night shift in Concord and was returning home to Clayton. On her approach to her home she witnessed what was said to have been a cigar shaped object glowing on the North side of Mt. Diablo. When she pulled into her drive she exited the car and took a seat on the front patio and observed the object for many minutes. It started at the far West side of Mount Diablo and was about half way up the mountainside. The object pulsated and moved in a perfectly straight line across the face of the mountain. If it were a car, the lights would have disappeared and reappeared behind trees and the trajectory of the object would have been irregular as it would have moved along the bumpy mountain terrain. The object took its time to move the whole length of the mountain, and then out of the blue, turned right back on itself and flew back the same direction it had just come from. In a state of disbelief at what she was witnessing, the lady popped in the house, got herself a beverage and thought nothing more of it.

Her curiosity got the better of her and she peeked once more out the window. The object was still scanning the side of the mountain. She returned outside and watched it for about ten minutes, then without warning, the object shot off into the heavens and was not seen again. Thinking she was seeing things, she contacted her father and explained what had just happened. He told her she was seeing things and it was time to go to bed. She went to bed and thought nothing more of what had happened. The following day, the evening paper had a headline that said "UFO seen on Devil's Mountain" or words to that effect. The newspaper article gave the same description that this lady had seen. It was validation enough for her. I have not been able to find the newspaper article from the 1960's.

35 - Black Bart Thank You Notes

This story was first told to me while touring a haunted location in Clayton. A young lady by the name of Jessica told me the story of an outlaw named Black Bart. She only knew the basics of the story, but put me in touch with a pair of brothers who had a lot of knowledge on this folklore. This is how this story goes: Charles Earl Bowles (b. 1829; d. after 1888), also known as Black Bart, was an English-born outlaw noted for the poetic messages he left behind after two of his robberies. He allegedly left thank you notes in the DeMartini Winery each time he broke in and stole bottles of wine.

He was considered a gentleman. Mr. Bowles was a Clayton school teacher and later in life became a well known bandit with a reputation for style and sophistication. He was one of the most notorious stagecoach robbers to operate in and around Northern California during the 1870's and 1880's.

On August 13, 1862, Bowles enlisted as a private in Company B, 116th Illinois Regiment (his name is spelled "Boles" in the company records). He was a good soldier and became the first sergeant within a year. Bowles was seriously wounded at the Battle of Vicksburg, and took part in Sherman's March to the Sea. He received brevet commissions as both second lieutenant and first lieutenant, and on June 7, 1865, was discharged with his regiment in Washington, D.C.

With many failed ventures during his early life including gold mining, he thought that there was a much easier way to make a living. On July 26, 1875, Bowles robbed his first stagecoach in Calaveras County, California. He netted one hundred sixty dollars, which was not a bad day's pay in those days.

He continued robbing until things started to turn sour for his ventures. The story goes as follows: His last holdup took place on November 3, 1883, at the site of his first robbery on Funk Hill, southeast of the present town of Copperopolis. Driven by Reason McConnell, the stage had crossed the Reynolds Ferry on the old road from Sonora to Milton. The driver stopped at the ferry to pick up Jimmy Rolleri, the nineteen-year-old son of the ferry owner. Rolleri had his rifle with him and got off at the bottom of the hill to hunt along the creek and meet the stage on the other side. When he arrived at the western end, he found that the stage was not there and began walking up the stage road. Near the summit, he saw the stage driver and his team of horses.

McConnell told him that as the stage had approached the summit, Bowles had stepped out from behind a rock with a shotgun in his hands. He forced McConnell to unhitch the team and take them over the crest of the hill. Bowles then tried to remove the strongbox from the stage, but it had been bolted to the floor and took some time to remove. Rolleri and McConnell went over the crest and saw Bowles backing out of the stage with the strong box. McConnell grabbed Rolleri's rifle and fired at Bowles twice, but missed. Rolleri took the rifle and fired as Bowles entered a thicket. He stumbled as if he had been hit. Running to the thicket, they found a small, blood-stained bundle of mail he had dropped.

Bowles' hand was wounded. After running a quarter of a mile, he stopped and wrapped a handkerchief around his hand to control the bleeding.

He found a rotten log and stuffed the sack with the gold amalgam into it, keeping five hundred dollars in gold coins. He hid the shotgun in a hollow tree, threw everything else away, and fled. In a manuscript written by stage driver, McConnell, about twenty years after the robbery, he claimed he fired all four shots at Bowles. The first missed, but he thought the second or third shot hit Bowles, and was sure the fourth did. Bowles only had the one wound to his hand.

When Bowles was wounded and forced to flee, he left behind several personal items.

Legend of Black Bart:
Poetic Stage Robber

These included his eyeglasses, some food, and a handkerchief with a laundry mark F.X.O.7. Wells Fargo Detective James B. Hume found these at the scene. Hume and detective Harry N. Morse contacted every laundry in San Francisco about the laundry mark. After visiting nearly ninety laundries, they finally traced it to Ferguson & Bigg's California Laundry on Bush Street and were able to learn that the handkerchief belonged to a man who lived in a modest boarding house.

The detectives learned that Bowles called himself a mining engineer and made frequent "business trips" that coincided with the Wells Fargo robberies. After initially denying he was Black Bart, Bowles eventually admitted he had robbed several Wells Fargo stages, though he confessed only to crimes committed before 1879. Bowles apparently believed the statute of limitations had expired on those robberies. When booked, he gave his name as T.Z. Spalding, but police found a Bible, a gift from his wife, inscribed with his real name.

It is believed that during his time in the boarding house in San Francisco, Black Bart would travel inland and find himself in Clayton, California. With the thrill of the bustling town filled with saloons and all sorts of adult entertainment, Black Bart still found a thrill in stealing instead of paying with all that loot he had collected over the years. He would leave the active down town area and make his way through the trees and approach what was a stunning three story building that was cut into the side of the hill and where two babbling brooks meet to flow northwards.

Folklore has it that Black Bart monitored the building from the heavy underbrush until the winery was locked up for the night. He then made his way to a side window and pry open the window frame to climb inside. He ensured there was no one else in the building, and would make his way to the storage area where found a comfortable spot and made his way through as many bottles of wine he was able to handle. Staggering to his feet, he stuffed full bottles into his jacket and made his way to the opened window. He took a few moments to pencil a thank you note and leave it where it would easily been seen. He exited the window with full bottles in tow. The window was then closed and Black Bart disappeared into the night.

Wells Fargo only pressed charges on the final robbery. Bowles was convicted and sentenced to six years in San Quentin Prison, but he was released after four years for good behavior. By January 1888, his health had deteriorated due to his time in prison; he had visibly aged, his eyesight was failing, and he had gone deaf in one ear. Rumor has it that local reporters swarmed around him when he was released and asked if he was going to rob any more stagecoaches. "No, gentlemen," he replied smiling, "I'm through with crime." Another reporter asked if he would write more poetry. Bowles laughed and said, "Now, didn't you hear me say that I am through with crime?"

Black Bart was last seen on February 28, 1888, when he disappeared from his hotel room, and was never seen again.

Bowles left only two authenticated verses. The first was at the scene of the August 3, 1877, holdup of a stage traveling from Point Arena to Duncans Mills, California, it read: "I've labored long and hard for bread, for honor and for riches, but on my corns too long you've tread, you fine-haired sons of bitches."

— Black Bart, 1877

The second verse was left at the site of his July 25, 1878, holdup of a stage traveling from Quincy to Oroville, California: "Here I lay me down to sleep to wait the coming morrow, perhaps success, perhaps defeat, and everlasting sorrow. Let come what will, I'll try it on, my condition can't be worse; And if there's money in that box, 'Tis munny in my purse."

— Black Bart

Even though Black Bart allegedly spent a very short amount of time in this area, I came across a news article that was published by Renee Wing in Clayton Chronicles, April, 2015. It shows a different, more historic, side of Black Bart. The article reads: "Everybody has stories and most people are happy to relate them. All one has to do is be willing to listen and record. My own family landed in Massachusetts from England via Holland in 1632. We have a Wing family museum, the Wing Fort House, in East Sandwich, and a very active Wing Family Association complete with yearly reunions, a family magazine, and a genealogy website.

We live and breathe family folklore. So, let me now relate to you one of my favorite stories originally collected in the early 1960's by my great aunt and then again by my cousin from the same source, great, great aunt Nellie herself, who was then in her mid-eighties. Most of the information comes directly from Nellie's dictation; however, I have added some additional details about the gentleman involved.

My great, great aunt Nellie attended business school, graduating with high recommendations in 1899, at a time when most young ladies were getting married and raising children, not entering the workforce. How did she have the funds to attend this school? In 1882, when she was six years old, she, along with her father, brother, and two sisters, lived in the Webb House on Second Street in San Francisco. Her mother had died in

Finland prior to the family's move to America. They all made the acquaintance of another resident of the establishment, a kind and rather dapper gentleman by the name of Charles Bolton; Nellie's father actually became good friends with him. Mr. Bolton, a mining engineer, made the Webb House his headquarters, but he was often away, presumably investigating mining prospects in the foothills. From time to time, when he returned, he slipped some money to young Nellie, money she tucked away for her future.

How did Mr. Bolton really acquire his money? He put a flour-sack with eye holes over his head, stood in the middle of dusty roads, stopped stagecoaches, and politely demanded their Wells Fargo boxes.

Charles Bolton was, in fact, Charles Boles, aka "Black Bart, the Po8" (poet). Black Bart wrote poetry, but history has recorded only a few lines. More were written, though, according to Nellie. There exists a short poem consisting of six lines, each one beginning with a letter of her name. From top to bottom one reads, "N-E-L-L-I-E." The poem is sweet and gentle, designed to delight the heart of a little girl."

Future more, the same story was told on a television show called "Mysteries of the Museum" (S6 Ep6) originally aired on 2/6/14, with a few additional words from the Jeffrey Richardson; the Autry Museum curator, where the rifle of Black Bart is on public display. There is also a life size image of Black Bart in the Wells Fargo museum in Sacramento California.

Two sides to a story always make for more entertaining folklore, don't you think?

36 - Pioneer Inn

The Pioneer Inn was a hotel from the 1860's to the 1990's, when it was turned into offices for a church. In 2013, it was sold to the city of Clayton. Here, ghosts have been seen carrying objects around, and visitors have been touched by spirits on their hands and shoulders. The church folks have not spoken openly about activity in the building. When it was a bar and a restaurant, there were reports of spirits touching the patrons and shadowy figures seen toward the back of the building and up in what is now the attic space and what was, before the fire; the second floor of the building.

I visited the new owners of the church and asked for a little of its past history. Inside the building you notice a very modern, well-kept interior with offices throughout. In the far north end you can see where extensions had been added to make room for a meeting space and on that day, a sewing club. The employee I spoke to made no mention of anything paranormal, but he did tell me some interesting facts about the structure of the building itself. History books and the Clayton Historical Society state the following on the Pioneer Inn:

"In 1857 (1858), a Frenchman named Romero Mauvais erected a house and then opened a tavern at the corner of Main and Center Streets. Many families made the hotel their home while building a permanent residence. The inn became known as the Clayton Hotel.

On February 28, 1864, disaster struck the budding town. Following an unprecedented drought in the winter of 1863-1864, most of the business district of Clayton was destroyed by fire, which began in the Clayton Hotel. Quoting from a March 5, 1864 article from the Contra Costa Gazette: "Henry Kerr, who was burned to death, was taken up to bed "drunk" by Mr. Barrow, the keeper of the Hotel. On returning to the bar room, Mr. Barrow found the paper of the wall behind the bar was on fire, and hurried to the pump to get water to put it out. The fire spread; the Hotel and the adjoining buildings were all made of wood, and in this dry season burned like tinder. The wind too was blowing quite fresh at the time. Thus the hotel and the butcher's shop and the stores of Messrs. Rhine and Clayton, lying next to the hotel on the east, were speedily consumed. Very little furniture and goods were saved. The fire spread and thus suddenly and without an hour's warning, there were eight houses with nearly all their contents totally consumed by fire. The total loss cannot fall short of about $15,000.00; the property was without insurance. This calamity is not without its lesson of warning to all our citizens. No one can be careful enough to guard against these accidents. The provident may take warning and get their houses and stores insured" (3/5/1864 Contra Costa Gazette).

The second level was put on the original Clayton Hotel, adding the six rooms that became the hotel. In 1868, this historic building was advertised as the first "concrete" Fireproof Mauvais' New Hall." Notices were published in the June 13, 1868, Contra Costa Gazette of "A Grand, Independence Ball at Clayton, on the evening of the 3rd of July 1868" which stated "A fine Band of Music has been engaged from San Francisco, and every arrangement will be made to insure the pleasure and satisfaction of guests. Tickets, including supper, $4.00." "No pleasanter or more accessible locality for a public gathering that the village of Clayton is to be found In the county, and the independence celebration there will attract a large attendance of our citizens generally."

After Zeno Mauvais (Romero Mauvias' son) sold the hotel to John Condie in 1875, this building became known as John Condie's Mt. Diablo Hotel. The building served as an inn and as a stopping point for the stage that ran from Stockton to the Bay Area.

In 1901, Antonio Nepolitano was the owner of the Mt. Diablo (Diablo) Hotel. After the original rock and mortar rear wall collapsed during an earthquake in June of 1901, it was replaced with a wooden frame construction; the other walls were protected from a like fate by timber reinforcing. Eventually the sign "Parlor" was removed from the front sitting room, and replaced by another sign that read "Post Office."

In 1946, Susan and Randall (Chubby) Humble purchased the restaurant/hotel that had become known as Tat's Place, and renamed it the Pioneer Inn. It became known throughout the region as a fine steak house, famous for fine food and celebrity diners. The kitchen was remodeled and a barbeque and copper hood made in 1950. In 1956, fire struck again. The second story was burned; customers saved all of the animal heads that had become a unique part of the Pioneer Inns' decor. The building was gutted, and the first floor was repaired and rebuilt, carefully saving a part of one of the old walls. A large dining room was added on the east side. Thick windowsills in the smaller dining room evidence some of the 1864 rock construction. The small dining room in back of the bar was the location of the 1940's post office.

John and Anita Jawad purchased the Pioneer Inn from Chubby Humble in 1964, and they continued to operate the famous steak house until failing health forced them to close the restaurant in the early 1990's.

In January 2002, the Clayton Community Church purchased the building to be used as church offices.

I was lucky enough to hear the story of the basement of this building which includes a series of huge old redwood support beams that run the length of the old structure. The beams are about two feet wide by about one foot deep and made of beautiful hard redwood. These beams were likely installed when the building was constructed in the mid 1800's. The beams themselves lay tightly on top of a hand-made wall of uneven rocks and mortar. The mortar appears fragile and is slowly crumbling away. The basement is original to when it was used as a beer and wine cellar. Right above the trapdoor is the location of the original bar that once stood near the front door of the hotel. The original bar is gone and it was replaced with a more modern bar and old photos of the location hang proudly on the walls. In the center of this set of photos is an incredible wooden panel that holds many of the local cattle brands burned into the wood. Over time it has been painted over, but you are still able to see the indentations of the markings.

Because it is a religious location and the belief in the paranormal is limited, I found it hard to verify any of the reports that have developed through the years. The head pastor of the church did tell me there was one incident that left him baffled. It took place within a few weeks of the purchase of the building. A church group decided that they would surround the building and offer prayer. Everything went well, until members started to drop out with severe headaches. Once people had disbanded and headed home, reports came in that almost everyone that was in the prayer circle suffered a headache.

Maybe the headaches were caused by spirits of the past when the location was used to a rough and tumble lifestyle with an active Brothel/Hotel scene. Perhaps they did not approve of the clean living lifestyle of the new tenants.

37- Losing Time in the Library

The local library in Clayton is a very new looking structure that sits on the site of the old Keller mansion barn. Reportedly, built over an ancient Miwok burial site, the library has seen its share of paranormal activity since it was constructed. The library has electric doors that stick as well as reports of heat spontaneously rising up through the floor. There have even been occurrences of clocks that; even after being synchronized, are reset to different times or are found to be running backwards. Patrons of the library feel the presence of a cold figure touching their hair or their arms as they sit in many different locations within the sprawling building.

After speaking with the staff, they confirmed that the site is on a Native American burial location, but many tribal leaders were asked to come into the area before building was allowed to take place. The leaders offered tribal rituals to allow the construction of the new library to begin. The staff members all state nothing unusual has happened to them since starting employment and most put the doors jamming to faulty electrics and the reason for the clocks stopping are dead batteries. The touching is also put down to a draft or air movement around people walking by.

38 - Two Bright Red Circular Objects

In January of 2016, a report was made to the National UFO Reporting Center regarding a sighting out of Clayton, California. It was headlined as two bright red circular objects that hovered brightly in one spot and then vanished. The report goes on to say: "Approximately 10:00 PM, my daughter and I were arriving home and facing north, when I noticed two circle objects that were reddish orange. They were different enough that I stopped the car and pointed them out to my daughter as possibly planets. She loves hearing about the stuff that goes on up there and at 5 loves the telescope. There were two when I first saw them and initially thought they were planets. With so many planets in sight soon, it was my initial thought because they weren't stars, shooting stars or airplanes clearly.

Then as I looked closer, I noticed they were the same exact shape and looked to be the same distance from myself, so being planets seemed impossible and the size was a little too large for a planet. One was a bit higher than the other one, but directly on top of it. It was an odd site at first. They were bigger than an airplane and it never blinked green or any other color. They both looked to burning brightly the more I looked at them, and luckily, there were planes in the sky that were somewhat nearby and those gave a quick way to compare and notice the obvious difference between the two.

I then quickly parked my truck and took my daughter to walk back to where we could see them. When we got back over there, it was maybe 1-2 minutes later, the highest one was gone and the lower one looked to be a little closer but pretty similar to its last position. When looking at it, I felt like it was moving although its position in the sky wasn't really changing much. It's hard to explain.

As I watched for another couple minutes, telling my daughter to watch it and pay attention, it didn't seem to brighten or dull much other than the thin, low flying clouds coming in between us at times, but never lost visibility of it. It sat there as bright as it had been and then quickly vanished. I couldn't explain it and thought, maybe clouds, but quickly saw another airplane fly in the same direction and it affirmed to me that it wasn't clouds and the quickness in which it disappeared affirmed to me that it wasn't the clouds that made it disappear from site. It wasn't an obstructed view; it disappeared from the sky; like it just turned off.

Although it wasn't doing much, it didn't seem like anything I'd ever seen. The bright glow compared to an airplane and the way it moved or even the way it didn't move was just odd and I'm a sky watcher so this is coming from someone who watches a lot and this was the first time I believed I'd seen something out of my realm of understanding."

Stories are reported on a steady basis in the area. There has never been any explanation from the local air bases.

39 - Pioneer Family Reunion

Two of the descendants of the pioneer families of the area offered a few stories of paranormal activity that had happened on their property. These cases were witnessed by others who confirmed the sightings. The first story begins with a couple who lived in a house on the top of the hill that once overlooked the downtown Clayton area. The house now sits on a large plot of land with a single story home sat back off of the road. With a "U" shaped driveway and so much beauty before your eyes, it is a wondrous place to visit. I was met at the front drive by their barking dog. We were waved in by the home owner and we made our way to the house that appeared to be built over ninety years ago. Beside the main house is another small house about thirty yards away. The small home was the last remaining part of one of the oldest homes in Clayton.

The small house has been renovated and is rented out and looks like a fine place to live.
The story begins while the two family members were inside the old house back in the 1977. One woman was in the kitchen area while the other woman was in the living room area. While cleaning dishes, the first woman saw what she thought was a family member standing in the doorway. What she was witnessing was her dead brother who had passed in November of 1972. She described the image as her brother with a huge grin on his face.

Without any doubt, he had returned to visit the ladies five years after his passing. As the one woman walked from the kitchen, she was stopped in her tracks and said

"Stuart!" This was validation for both of the ladies to prove this was the spirit of a dead brother had made an appearance to both of the women. When I asked what he looked like, I was told he appeared in the solid form with a slight haze around him. She described it "As if you were looking at someone through a screen door." As the ladies approached the entity, he faded away, but he returned a few more times over the years.

Other deceased family members have been seen inside the house over the years in the form of aunts and uncles and parents.

The homeowners' grandpa appeared in the front garden one afternoon. Another family member lived just down the street was stunned to witness what he thought was a ghost. He was heard yelling and screaming that he saw grandpa in the front yard of the ladies home. One of the ladies heard the commotion and came to the front door of the small cottage. Peering out, she was shocked by what she saw. Standing there as clear as a bell, with his coveralls on and a hoe in his hand stood her grandfather, just smiling away. The cousin came running down the street in the direction of the cottage and on to the property. By the time he arrived, his grandpa had vanished. The cousin was in total shock at what he had witnessed, so much so he was left pale and in a state of confusion. There was no way to prove what they saw, but both of them were sure of what they saw. The people in the area sat around for hours after the event discussing what they had witnessed and trying to explain away the vision. Many members of their family come back and 'visit' the homestead on a regular basis. They always smile and offer a feeling that they are in a good place and are happy in death.

The next incident occurred when one of the ladies was cleaning up trash from recent tenants that had lived in the larger of the two residences on the property. She heard the screen door open and slam shut. She assumed someone was coming around to visit, so she investigated. Once she approached the front door, she looked across to the other house, and, standing near the patio was her long deceased grandmother. "She was so real" she said. She knew who this was as they were very close during her childhood and she was by her grandma's bedside when she died.

The other family member senses there are people in the house and around the property at all times. This seems to be one of the more active locations in the town, but due to protect its privacy, the location will remain concealed from the general public.

40 - Blood in the Museum

On a recent interview I did with some members of the Historical Society and local historians, I heard a story that I believe had not been shared before.
As we sat around a patio table with three members of the museum, Jenny, and our daughter, Corlis, it was reported that during the remodeling of the museum, the workers did not enjoy being in the building after dark as strange feelings would consume them. They experienced a myriad of strange unexplainable sounds coming from inside what used to be the city founders original home. The home is connected to a second pioneer home to make for a larger museum space. The sounds of footsteps have been heard walking the second floor, there were cold spots moving around and

unexplained voices.

Most of the members of the staff are non-believers when it comes to anything paranormal; the idea of a ghost in Mr. Clayton's home sounds crazy. There was one skeptic who had a strange incident that was unexplainable.

It was during the renovation of what is now known as the Kid's Corner of the museum. This area is tucked away, in the middle of the museum, but what was once the back corner of one of the two homesteads. The walls were painted a nice clean white and objects were being brought in for the younger visitors of the museum to play with and to handle. It's an area where children can play without their parents freaking out that they have gotten their sticky paws on something valuable to the community and American history in general. With the construction well under way, there were a total of three people involved.

Once everything had been constructed, it was time to bring in objects such as an electric type writer and a Morse code machine. When the objects were brought into the room, the workers noticed fresh blood drops on the newly painted surface. All three staff members looked at their hands and arms to see who had cut themselves. To their dismay, no one had cut themselves and none of them were bleeding. They had no idea where the blood droplets came from or who was responsible for them. There was no one else in the building and the blood was fresh.

The staff stated that there was no injury to anyone and there was no logical explanation for the blood. Added to the accounts of footsteps and voices within the home, it indicates something strange might be happening. As a former paranormal investigator and a mega skeptic, I understand the way that outside voices and footsteps can appear inside of a home, but I have no way of explaining blood on freshly painted shelves.

I have had only one experience that occurred during an interview I was doing with Richard Ellis; a Joel Clayton historian. The discussion had turned to the writing of this book. I sat on a chair in the back room when, what felt like a person, came charging up and pushed past me while I was seated. I was struck so hard that it caused me, and the chair I was sitting in, to shift and the chair scuffed the hard wood floor. It was a very uneasy moment and as I looked around and there was no one behind me. I have no idea what it was.

41 - The Gomez House

The following is Clayton's most well known ghost story, and biggest mystery.

On August 25, 1957, the Oakland Tribune wrote a story on one of the more well-known paranormal reports from the City of Clayton. The story started in a small single-story home on Oak Street. The house was built on the site of the old jail, before the jail was moved to the other side of the road.

A few of the main characters involved with this

story were: Vic Chapman, the town's police constable; Tony and Mary Gomez, the owners of the home; and Tommy and Bobby Gomez, their young grandsons. After purchasing the house in 1928, Tony and Mary lived a peaceful existence with their six sons and three daughters in the three-bedroom home. School was within walking distance which made things much easier for the mother to get the kids out of the house. When the older kids moved out and started lives of their own, the mother of Tommy and Bobby handed the upbringing of the two boys to her parents. The mother had come by the house and told Mary and Tony that she was dropping off the boys and would be back to pick them up. She was never seen again.

On a warm summer's day while Mary was hanging freshly washed clothes on the line to dry, she started to get pelted with rocks, stones and mud balls. With a great amount of anger, she accused the two young boys of throwing the stones at her. The two boys plead innocent and said they were near the creek on the other side of the street. The attention and anger was then put on the Chapman kids, Sally and Butch that lived next door and often played with the Gomez boys. The children were confronted by Mrs. Gomez pounding on their front door. The two children said they were not outside and were not throwing rocks; they were elsewhere when the incident happened. Of course, the blame was then laid back on the two boys that were outside playing in the creek. Not much more came of it and was put down to childish pranks.

A few weeks passed, not much else happened in the neighborhood so the incident was forgotten. But later, more and more rocks started hitting the home. The windows were broken and at one point a brick came crashing through a pane of glass and landed in the middle of the living room floor. Enroy Gomez still lived close by in Concord and visited his parents on a regular basis at this time. He is quoted in newspaper reports saying that strange things started to happen within the walls of this homestead.

One reported example came when Enroy was visiting his family and everyone was sitting in the living room. The two boys were visible in the kitchen playing on the floor. Out of the blue, at around ten o'clock at night, the walls of the house started to shake and it sounded like someone was beating on the walls with a giant baseball bat. They assumed it was the neighbors pranking the family, so Enroy and the boys hurried outside to see what was causing all the commotion. Once outside, there was no one to be found. Immediately, the three members of the Gomez family made their way towards the Garbarino house that was up the hill. They thought that maybe someone was using some form of catapult to launch large rocks down on the house. But as they trekked up the hill they themselves started to get hit with smaller rocks that appeared to come out of the skies. This caused the three of them to flee and take cover. Enroy glanced over his shoulder, and the street lights lit up what looked like a thousand rocks hurtling through the air in all directions. The incident was reported to the mild mannered local constable, Vic Chapman, but very little was done to investigate the happenings of that night. Some of the other local kids in the neighborhood said it was more likely a revenge attack by the other kids for what the Gomez boys had done to them while out playing near the creek. The Gomez boys were well known for throwing mud wads at other kids and at people's homes during this period of time. Enroy was later interviewed and recorded saying what he heard and saw was the gospel truth, and there was no doubting his statements.

A week or two later, the paranormal activity took an unexpected turn for the worse. The house started to create a sad feeling and the family waited for the next series of suspicious activity to happen. Vic Chapman was asked to monitor the home and see who was throwing the rocks that caused material and physical damage. Chapman recruited a few good men to monitor the home, night and day. The men would hide out in the trees, bushes and up on the hill overlooking the property, but still the stones rained down. There was never a culprit identified in these attacks. In fact, there was never anyone around when it happened. Only bystanders that were unfortunate enough to pass the house that would end up getting injured by the flying projectiles. But after a day of the posse being seen in the neighborhood, the rocks stopped flying and the neighborhood became peaceful once again.

Even though outside had calmed down, the activity started picking up inside the home. One evening the family sat quietly and watched television, when a stuffed dog that sat on top of the television set flew off as if it was being thrown. It did not just fall on the floor; it was as if someone threw it across the room. This startled everyone that witnessed it, seconds later the sound of things hitting the floor in the kitchen was heard. As the family members entered the kitchen, the salt shaker flew around the room in a wild pattern. A pan came crashing off the shelf and onto the floor. Mrs. Gomez bent down to pick up the skillet, but was hit with flying onions and potatoes from the kitchen table. It was enough to have the family believe that they were the owners of a haunted house and they attributed the recent activity to something paranormal; perhaps some unhappy poltergeist. A few days passed and the family lived in fear of what would happen next. Then one night when Mrs. Gomez entered the kitchen, a box of salt flew off of the table and struck her square in the back causing her to stumble forward.

The local constable was outside patrolling the

area when this incident had occurred and noticed something unusual. The constable was positioned in the back yard with his back to the home when he heard a very loud banging on the wood siding of the house. Spinning around and expecting to see a culprit in action, he saw no one. Running around the front of the home, there was no one around and the streets were empty of any passersby. Using his radio, he asked if the posse had seen anyone around the area moments before. They all said they had not seen anyone in the area for almost thirty minutes. The streets were very quiet that night.

Then with a loud smash, a window broke and within a few seconds a package from the kitchen flew out of the freshly broken pane. "The window broke on its own, and the package that was on the center of the table, started to move, then shot out of the broken window" was how the family explained this incident. There was a trophy that sat proudly on a shelf beside a small lamp in the living room. This trophy only ever moved when Mrs. Gomez would dust the area but on this day the trophy flipped off and landed about three feet in front of its starting spot. It is alleged that a pot fell from the sink and then jumped back into its original location. There was also a report of a fountain pen leaping from the arm of one rocking chair and levitating down the hallway to come to rest on another rocking chair in another room.

On a separate occasion, a cigarette ashtray came crashing through a window barely missing Mr. Gomez as he sat quietly on his front porch. The younger Mr. Melvin Gomez contacted the University of California to ask for a scientific explanation of the phenomenon. The elders of the home started to show signs of stress and worry from all this activity that happened around them. Mary started to lose a lot of weight and Tony refused to fix any of the now fifteen broken windows on the property. The couple lost interest in life and wanted to just sit around and be left alone.

Rumor has it that the original land plot belonged to a Frenchman named Pioche. We are not sure if it's the same wealthy businessman that Pioche Nevada was named after. He found his fate in the dark streets of San Francisco when he was brutally murdered in what was believed to be a robbery. His land was then reclaimed and homes were built on the land claim. Perhaps the unexplained occurrences were inflicted by the spirit of the Frenchman who was upset about something that was going on within the four walls of the Gomez house. Perhaps it was just the detailed imagination of someone wanting to be famous.

There is also a report of a young boy that was shot to death on the property when the boy hid a gun in the washing that hung on the line of clothes. The sixteen year old was spotted chopping wood across the street but approached the washing line and retrieved the gun. The boy then walked behind the constable and fired off two shots, both missing their intended target. The constable spun around and returned one shot that found its target sending the youth to the ground and killing him on the spot. It was believed that the father of the boy knew what his son intended to do that day, but did nothing to stop him. A few of the neighbors stated that the boy had it coming to him as he was not a model citizen. Maybe the unexplained activity was a form of ghostly payback from the boy. Perhaps they are the acts of a departed coward who had a run in with the law at one of the local saloons that lined the streets of Clayton. We will never know. After the newspaper report, the small town of Clayton was flooded with tourists wanting to have a glimpse of the "Spook House." So much so, that the main streets through the town were lined with cars and people wandered around with cameras. One positive was that this was a great boost to the community and the local economy of the time.

For the past sixty years there have been no reports of any paranormal activity at the home. The house is now rented out to long time tenants that have claimed no paranormal activity at all. This story has been told in almost all the local newspapers throughout the area. Every few years it appears again in print. Samples were taken from The Oakland Tribune, Contra Costa Times, SF Examiner and Chronicle and Clayton Pioneer to help write this story.

42 - La Veranda Café / Utley House

On the intersection of Marsh Creek Road and

Center Street, in Clayton, opposite from "The Grove" park, sits a wonderful Italian restaurant. Decked out with clean white and gray paint and a wrap-around balcony, this building is an image of the old west in its structural design. This short story comes from a few of the locals that have lived in the town and knew the building before it became a restaurant. Behind the building are the remains of foundations from a home that once stood on the other side of the creek. The home on the site; was known as the Utley Home. Locals reported playing in the house when the Utleys lived there.

They experienced doors opening and closing as well as unexplained knocking on walls. A few of the locals recall being in the home they heard a knock on the front door. The father walked and unlatched the door to see who was outside. The door burst open and sent him toppling backwards. The kids then experienced what they described as a cold spot that moved around the room and exited. As it left, the door slammed shut. There have also been reports of a lady seen rocking in a chair behind the parking lot.

This lady has been seen on many occasions; due to the realistic appearance of this spirit, people believe it's a lady in costume. From reports, she appears in 1850's style clothing, with her head covered in a shawl or a bonnet. She stares off into the water as it rushes by. She steadily rocks back and forth waiting for what is believed to be the return of her young child that drowned on the spot many years before. The mother was in so much grief, that within a year of her child's death, she passed away. On special occasions she is seen at the end of the parking lot, nestled in the trees. If you ascend the hill on Center Street, you can peek over the bridge and into the shaded area by the stream. You may see the sad mother down there, waiting for her missing child to return.

43- Gathering Place Pranks

With the arrival of spring and with all the available chapters of the book completed and proofread, I was prepared to focus back on my schooling and try and make some sort of a living.

Our daughter is in Daycare and one of my daily tasks is to get her up and ready for school. I have been taking her every day for several months. One day, when I was in the parking lot of her school, I was approached by a woman that said she had a great story connected with a gathering spot in Clayton and wanted to see if I was interested in it for this book. She stated there was a lot of activity in a nearby building but all of a very positive nature.

While propped up against the fence, I broke out my note pad and pen, items I always carry with me just in case a story comes my way. She stated she was the manager of this other location and when she started working she was responsible for locking up the building at the end of her shift. All other staff would had left by this time of day. As the front door was locked, she glanced back into the darkened building only to see a light had turned itself back on. After turning off the light for a second time, she left for home.

The light turned on and off once in a while, but wasn't a concern as it did not harm anyone. Sometimes, the manager showed up for work before any other staff members were there, only to find different lights turned on overnight.

She reported hearing voices inside a room just around the corner from the main lobby area. It sounded like the voices were coming from the room beside her. Her interest was piqued as she thought she was alone in the building. She peered through the large window into the room from which the voices were coming. The room was dark and there was no one there. She could clearly hear the voices for a few minutes more before they faded away. Voices have been reported in the building on other occasions and in different locations throughout.

There are a lot of reports of doors opening on their own even though the building has a system that does not allow for easy opening by the wind or simple pressure. A perfect example of this was a few days before this story was written when the manager was talking to a staff member to make sure she got the story for me. She said they were both in a room alone when the discussion of the ghosts came up. She said within a few minutes things started falling off the shelves, items that had not moved in years hit the floor. Then to their surprise, the bathroom door swung open then slammed shut. The staff believes there is more to the occurrences than a loose light fitting or a gust of wind.

One night, a few of the staff offered to debunk the happenings, but were unable explain any of the occurrences that had happened. Voices were replicated but it was obvious that there were people standing in the other room.

The previous manager also experienced what they thought was a very friendly spirit in the building. There was never any worry for the staff as whatever was there is seemed to be enjoying itself. The original site was cleansed by Native Americans before the building was constructed. There was no form of burial on the site, even though it was close to many other spots that contained burials.

As an after note I add this next chapter, as I found out that since the conversations between staff members regarding the ghosts in the building, the spirit activity has increased. The day after we did our interview for the book, the manager was locking up the building and she started to hear what sounded like people talking. It was not isolated to just one spot; it seemed like it was all around her. This was enough to spook her. As she walked down a long hallway, the sounds got louder. As she got to the noisy room, the lights in the hallway turned on without any help from her. This was enough to scare her and she called her husband to come get her. Upon his arrival, the lights continued turning on and off. The couple then heard what sounded like heavy tools crashing to the ground in the back part of the building. The husband gingerly made his way down the long hallway, but there was nothing on the floors in any of the rooms. Everything was neatly put away. The building became silent once again and the husband returned to the front doors. The light switched on again and the manager turned it off then they left in a hurry.

The following morning, everything was back to normal. The uneasy feeling and the electrical charge that the couple experienced the night before was gone. The morning brought the normal happy vibes of day to day operation.

I have a feeling there will be a lot more activity

in this location; but as long as it remains calm there will be no problem. If things get too bad, I will have one of my close friends help me out. Cindy Riggs is an internationally known Psychic, Spiritual Mentor, Universal Channel and Defrag-Mentor. She is able to help with unwanted hauntings and helps the living deal with the paranormal. There are very few people I personally trust in the field of the paranormal; Cindy is by far the best. You can contact her at Cindyriggs.com. This address of this location will not be disclosed. They do not want visitors walking in and bothering them with questions while they are working.

44- Pizza Shop Observations

As I was preparing to finish up writing this book, I had realized that I had missed a few very important locations in the town. These buildings have been through many changes over the years and I was sure there was a story or two in these locations. After offering a speaking engagement at the Historical Society and meeting with Richard Taylor to tie down a few loose ends when it came to this book, I made my way to the local pizza shop. It's a very well known location in Clayton and it offers a fantastic pizza, beer, video games and sports on the big screen.

I made my way into the location at around 4:30 PM and the place was already hopping with activity. The phone was ringing off the hook with orders and people were starting to line up to pick up previously ordered food.

I tried to get a few answers to my questions between the mad rushes of people. I was told the manager was out on a run and would not be back for twenty minutes. The young girl at the front desk said there was a lot of paranormal activity within the building but she was too busy to supply details. I fully respected this and was prepared to return another day, but as I was preparing to leave an employee by the nickname of "Tobi" said he would share a few stories with me.

We walked to the very back of the building where there was a small room that contained many video games. This room is out of the way but is monitored with cameras throughout. Tobi told me that he was responsible for wiping down all the machines and for cleaning the windows in this building. He said, one day he had just finished closing the game room at approximately 9:45 PM. He had locked the doors and proceeded to wash down the windows. Once the windows were completed, he moved to the glass doors; one in front and one in back; then once the windows were dried, he headed into the bathroom.

After a period of time he emerged from the bathroom with cleaning supplies in hand, and noticed there was a hand print of a child about three feet from the floor. He thought it was on the outside of the glass and unlocked the door to clean the print off. As he started to scrub he realized that this print was on the inside of the door. He reentered the game room and reached down and wiped off the small hand print.

This was very puzzling to the young man, so he went and asked to review the surveillance video from the game room while he was in there cleaning. The manager and he reviewed the footage and saw no child inside the room and no sign of anyone touching the glass door panel. The hand print had appeared out of thin air without any warning.

There are more reports of activity near the front of the building with stories of the back exit that leads out to the rear patio door being held closed when staff wishes to pass through it. The lock on the door is in an open position and the door swings open easily. This enables the staff to lean into it so they can carry trays of food and drink out to the patrons without any real effort. But sometimes this door is stuck closed by some unseen force. After a few pushes, the door flies open, allowing the staff to continue their chores. I suggested it could be the wind pushing against the door, but I was reminded that the door would be slightly ajar when this happens. If a wind was involved, it would blow the door shut and cause the latch to engage.

Recently, two young staff members were in the main building cleaning off tables as one of the girls glanced back in the direction of the other; she witnessed a person right behind her friend. The girl asked if there was any way they could help the patron, but the figure disappeared.

The manager is aware of some paranormal activity in the building and staff members refuse to lock up on their own and always want have to have someone with them. There is a feeling that the building gets heavy and eerie when the lights go out at the end of the night.

So if you ever decide to stop for a pizza in Clayton, you must make a stop at Skipolini's Pizza and buy one of the best pizza pies in the State, and don't forget to look out for the spirits that roam the building.

45- Salon's Friendly Spirit

If you take a walk down Main Street in Clayton, you will more than likely miss the Frontier Salon. This location sits back off of the main road and houses its parking lot in front of what appears to be a residence. By the look of the single story property, you can tell this is part of Clayton's historic past. The home was owned by the Bloching family and finally converted into a salon. It has been passed through many hands and is now run by Shelley B.

The original structure burned down when electricity was brought to the town. Many people had no idea of the dangers from fire and many buildings succumbed to flame due to poor wiring and their wooden frames. This location was rebuilt and remains in its original position. The only major changes to the building include a lot of stucco and stone work added to the original wood during its time as a flower shop, clothing store and doctor's office.

I was lucky to be able to interview the owner in between haircut appointments. Their reaction was very positive toward sharing the stories of the building. When Shelley first met the previous owner to discuss the site, she asked if there was anything she needed to know about the building. The previous owner responded with "Everything is OK with the exception of Harold." It seems that Harold was the name given to the spirit that haunts the location. Harold is known to turn lights on and off, slam doors and move items around the building. In the past, voices were heard but that has not occurred since the new tenant has taken over the location. Shelly has experienced doors slamming but put it all down to Harold. The building was cleansed by Pastor Shawn; this may be a reason for less recent activity now than before. Whatever is in the building is not causing any harm or concern to anyone and appears to do its own thing. It may be residual in nature and have no idea that there are living souls around when it starts moving items. Please respect the privacy of this location as it is hard to answer questions and cut and dye hair all at the same time.

46- The Royal Rooster Gift Shop

As many of these stories come to me via rumor or by second and third party, this is one of those that was direct and had happened the day I entered the shop to request an interview. When it comes to paranormal experiences, I have had many experiences over my ten years of working in the field. I have hosted haunted locations, led investigations, and worked with television production companies for paranormal television shows.

One thing that I have experienced is an uneasy feeling; it is a feeling of dread. I become short of breath, and sometimes sweaty. It is like a panic attack, I have no control and there is no reason why I feel that way. Once I walked into this lovely Clayton gift and home décor shop, I got that uneasy feeling. On my first trip into the store, I met Abby. Abby is a young lady with a very pleasant disposition. She greeted me from behind the counter and asked if she could be of assistance to me. I told her why I was there and that a few neighboring businesses said I should stop by.

I explained the premise of this book and with a sly smile she said that I was there just in time. She had just experienced what sounded like a loud pop or bang that came from one corner of the store. It was loud enough to get the attention of the customers in the store. Abby investigated the area the noise came from, but found nothing amiss. She put this down to yet another strange occurrence of many that started around Christmas of 2015.

I also met with a young woman named Katie who has witnessed many of these instances during her time working in the store. On my second trip to the business, I was immediately struck with a feeling of sadness and doom the second I walked in the door. I sank into a panic attack within seconds. The room felt heavy and overbearing to me as I tried to catch my breath. Chatting with these lovely ladies should have been an easy task for me, but for some reason, I found myself struggling with basic questions that I ask every day. What I learned from the interviews was a series of strange happenings that left these two ladies and the owner; Sarah, scratching their heads in disbelief.

One story, told by both the staff members, included the sound of items being moved and shuffled around in a secluded corner of the store. They also reported the sound of someone stocking shelves. When the staff made their way to the corner, the sounds stopped and nothing appeared out of place. During other times the sound of people walking around are heard when the store was empty. Like many locations in Clayton, they report lights being turned off and the flickering of different sets of lights throughout the store. The ladies also experienced the feeling of being watched or someone looking over their shoulder.

One day the owner; Sarah, was checking someone's purchases out at the register when she had the feeling someone was rubbing against her. Of course, there was nobody there, but what startled her most was that whatever it was reached across her back and grabbed her shoulder in a hugging motion. Not wanting to scare the customer, she played it off at the time, but it felt real and scared her into thinking her building was defiantly haunted.

Over the Christmas period, Katie had brought in all the items that were on display outside the front doors of the store. The store was closing for the night and all items were carefully placed on the floor near the door. Katie admitted she was a bit clumsy when it came to moving items, but she swore this evening she laid everything neatly on the floor, out of the way of the doorway. The building was locked up for the night and everyone went home. In the morning when Sarah unlocked the store, she noticed that an angel display was smashed as if it was dropped from some height. Pieces lay all over the floor, but Katie said she did not break the angel. If she would have she would have cleaned up the mess and reported it to the boss. She did not smash the angel, and did not know who did or how this could happen. Another report came from Abby; she was also closing up shop for the night when she placed a cake plate on a table near the front doors. The doors were locked and everyone left for the night. In the morning the plate was found with a clean break right through the center. It was still in the same position Abby had left it, but was now broken in half.

The most intriguing happening was when both Abby and Katie were locking up the building and Abby was in the center of the floor. Katie had walked towards the back of the store and turned to see Abby in the same spot but now there was a male figure inches behind her. Katie was shocked by what she saw and within a split second the man was gone. Abby said she sometimes feels like she is being watched from a distance; this causes a very uneasy feeling for all the females in the store. The location was once a family home and after tracking down the family connection, I was told there were never any strange happenings when they lived there.

Whatever this is has visited since the 1950s and is makes itself known today. It seems to be harmless, even though it does scare the girls once in a while but they feel no danger. If you are in Clayton, I encourage you to visit the store and purchase a few items for your home. Maybe you will experience the sound of things moving on the shelves.

47- Marsh Creek and Main

There have been reports of strange looking

figures seen on the edge of "The Grove" at the intersection of Main Street and Marsh Creek Road. Many police reports have been made of a child out very late at night, just standing on the corner looking lost. Could this be "Molly" from my previous account or is this someone new? Maybe the drowned child from across the street or an unidentified spirit who's story is yet to be told. There is very little known about this child spirit who hangs around the site of the old eucalyptus grove that once grew in what is now the city park.

This site, close to the iconic city clock, is rumored to be haunted by Judge Goethal. Rumor has it that within view of his home, he was tragically killed when his buggy hit a rut and flipped over on him, crushing him. This story is not true as the newspaper reports from the 1920's state he died of old age in San Francisco and was buried in Antioch CA. It does appear that he lived in the home which is now one half of the Chophouse restaurant. He is said to wander the area from the corral to the grove and up to his former home. His image is often seen in the still of the night when there is little or no traffic on the roads.

The final story I have is that of a rancher corralling horses close to the corral area. He has only been reported a few times and many of these reports were from before 1980. I cannot find any recent reports of sightings of the man and his animals. This was one of the areas where horses would have been tied when miners and ranchers entered town for supplies and entertainment.

48- Morgan Territory Dead Can Talk

Morgan Territory is a secluded and very rough terrain location on the outskirts of the City of Clayton. It is a perfect place to dump a body and have it remain hidden for a long time. There have been reports of people being driven to the area and murdered or have their bodies dumped here after being killed elsewhere. One of the bodies that were found here was connected to an area serial killer and broke open the case. Credit is given to Crimezzz.net for the following article. Many of the victims from this case were not found in the Clayton area, but the one body that was found on Morgan Territory was the one that convicted this mass murder.

The report reads:

"Phillip Joseph Hughes, Jr., is serving concurrent life sentences for killing three young women in the early 1970s, but investigators believe he may be responsible for other killings, including a 15-year-old Moraga girl who vanished in 1970.

The body of Cosette Ellison was identified by a then-new technique using an X-ray of the bones in her hand. Her case also has drawn in an old high school friend, now a BART police officer, who has been working with investigators.

Nearly a dozen girls and young women disappeared or were killed in Alameda and Contra Costa counties from 1969 to 1979. Hughes is at the top of the suspect list in at least seven of those cases.

"Philip Hughes was convicted of three homicides, but I'm 100 percent positive he is responsible for much more than that," said Paul Holes, supervising criminologist for the Contra Costa Sheriff's forensic services division.

For any unsolved case from the late 1960s until the time of his arrest (in 1980), he will be considered until he's eliminated as a person of interest.

One of the earliest victims on the unsolved list, Ellison disappeared after school on March 3, 1970. She was a sophomore at Campolindo High, the same school Hughes and one of his victims, 19-year-old Maureen Field, attended. Like Field, who vanished in November 1972, Ellison's body was found in a ravine off Morgan Territory Road, south of Clayton.

Two of the three women Hughes was convicted of killing were petite brunettes. Like Ellison and many of the victims on the unsolved case list; most lived in the Lamorinda (The name is a portmanteau from the names of the three cities that make up the region: **La**fayette, **Mor**aga and Or**inda**.) and Walnut Creek area, others were from Rodeo and San Pablo.

Hughes, who is serving his time at the California Men's Colony in San Luis Obispo, didn't respond to several Times requests for an interview.

In 1980, Hughes was convicted of the 1974 stabbing death of 15-year-old Lisa Ann Beery of Oakland; the 1972 stabbing and strangulation of Field, a Pleasant Hill resident; and the 1975 murder of Letitia Fagot, 25, of Walnut Creek.

Police arrested Hughes, a 31-year-old janitor, after his wife, Suzanne Perrin, told Oakland police in July 1979 about the slayings, bringing an end to seven years of sadomasochistic sex rituals and rape murders.

Perrin testified during Hughes' trial that he wanted to kill a former girlfriend, but feared he was an obvious suspect, so he killed others in place of the petite brunette. "He wanted it to be someone who was close to Cathy's build and looks," Perrin testified. His wife confessed to helping her husband dispose of the bodies of Beery and Field, and to giving Hughes the names of four female coworkers, including Fagot, as "possible victims for murder." She received immunity from prosecution for her testimony. Field, the first victim among Hughes convictions, disappeared Nov. 14, 1972 after work at a Pleasant Hill K-Mart. Her body was found four months later. She had been stabbed and strangled.

Hughes and Perrin kidnapped Beery at knife point near her Montclair home on Jan. 26, 1974. The couple took her to an Oakland home where they were house-sitting and Perrin waited upstairs while Hughes stabbed and raped the Oakland choir girl. Police found her body, with Perrin's help, buried on a Rheem hillside in July 1979.

Fagot, Perrin's coworker at the French Bank of California in San Francisco, was found dead in her Los Cerros Avenue home in Walnut Creek on March, 19, 1975. She had been strangled with a cord and bludgeoned with a hammer.

In 1980, Hughes was sentenced to three concurrent terms of 21 years to life in prison. At the time, California's capital punishment law was not in effect and juries didn't have the option of recommending life in prison without parole. Hughes has been eligible for parole since 1986.

On July 25, 2001, a parole board gave Hughes a

five-year denial of parole, the maximum allowed, after a hearing where representatives of the victim's families spoke.

Hughes hasn't participated in prison self-help opportunities or therapy since 1993 and psychiatric reports don't support his release. One commissioner said the reports concluded Hughes has no feelings for others and no idea of society's norms. "As soon as Phil came forward lots of cases were lumped at him," Holes said. After his arrest, more than 15 California police agencies asked to question him regarding unsolved cases.

Just as new technology helped police identify Cosette, recent advances in DNA testing eliminated Hughes as a suspect in some cases, such as the 1978 strangulation of Armida Wiltsey at the Lafayette Reservoir.

In 2000, the crime lab notified detectives they now had the equipment to test evidence from the Wiltsey case. The next year, the lab ruled out Hughes as a source of the male DNA found underneath her fingernails.

But, while Hughes has been cleared in some

cases, he remains a person of interest in seven others:

• Leona Roberts, 16, was last seen Nov. 10, 1969 in front of her boyfriend's apartment on Tormey Road in Rodeo. Her body was found at Bolinas Lagoon near Point Reyes on Dec. 28, 1969.

• Elaine Davis, 17, disappeared while baby-sitting her 3-year-old sister at their Pioneer Avenue home in Walnut Creek on Dec. 1, 1969. A body found floating off Light House Point in Santa Cruz in 1969 was exhumed in May 2001 and identified as Davis using dental records.

• Ellison was last seen about 3:30 p.m. March 3, 1970 in the driveway of her Canyon Road home in Moraga. Her remains were found Jan. 1, 1971 in a ravine off of Morgan Territory Road.

• Patricia King, 25, was found near the football stadium at Diablo Valley College in Pleasant Hill on March 5, 1970. She was strangled with her leggings after an evening exercise class.

• Lisa Dickinson, 9, disappeared Sept. 5, 1976 while riding her bike from her home on Los Cerros Avenue in

Walnut Creek toward Heather Farms Park. Her bike was found leaning against a tree inside the park, but the girl has never been found.

• Lou Ellen Burleigh, 21, of Walnut Creek vanished Sept. 11, 1977 on her way to a job interview at a Pleasant Hill shopping center on Contra Costa Boulevard.

• Tara Cossey, 9, was last seen while walking to the Pirelli's Liquor store in San Pablo to purchase a bag of sugar for her mother on June 6, 1979.

"Their families don't have closure, there's no justice," Holes said. "It always burns me that these people think they got away with it."

And there are the victims themselves.

"You see a picture of Cosette and you feel something," Holes said. "There's something that catches you -- they were robbed of life."

In the 1970s, other serial killers were at work in Northern California including the Zodiac and the I-5 Strangler, Roger Kibbe, but Holes isn't convinced that

Hughes was inactive from 1975 until his arrest five years later.

"There's very little crime in the Walnut Creek and Lamorinda areas," Holes said. "To me, it's more than a coincidence that housewives and young girls turned up missing or dead in a common area."

Sgt. Steve Warne, supervising investigator with the Sheriff's Office homicide division, said detectives periodically review cold cases, especially those most likely to be solved with new and developing technology.

It was a chance sighting of a poster marking some of that new technology used in the Ellison case that led Kim Garner, her friend and former classmate, to lend her knowledge to the investigation.

Ellison's body had been the first in Contra Costa to be identified using X-ray comparisons and the poster was created to commemorate the milestone

"Pretty much everything that exists in that case is related to the evidence. If there's some new technology that can develop any leads we'll dig back into it," he said.

"One more case could keep Hughes in jail," Hole said.

Another folklore tale tells of a rancher who went to the Concord area to recruit day labor for his farm. He picked up the workers and drove them back to his ranch near Morgan Territory. He had them work the day and instead of paying them a wage and returning them to Concord, he butchered them and dumped their remains in the woods that surrounded the area. This went on for over a year, with many illegal workers being murdered. Because these men were illegal, no one ever reported the missing bodies. It was kept quiet. It was not brought to the surface until a pair of hikers got off track and stumbled on the skeletal remains of a man in coveralls. It was later discovered that many of the men had been shot in the back and dragged the short distance from the ranch.

49- Daytime UFO

West of Town was the site of a daytime UFO

experience. In broad daylight, this object was seen from Clayton Road. Here is the report to SOTT.net:

"This morning, around 11 AM, I received this photo of something in the skies above CLAYCORD, along with the following message....

"I saw this object in the sky in South Concord looking towards Clayton today and I have no idea what it is. I was standing in my back yard and my daughter pointed it out. When I first saw it, it looked like it actually went down, then up again. By the time I went inside to get my camera it was gone, then we found it again on the other side of the sky." The photograph was not connected to this report and there is no proof of this image in the UFO files of SOTT.net

The second report stated:

"I actually saw it, too, while on Clayton Road this morning. It was lower though, and it definitely wasn't a helicopter like we've seen these past few days flying over Concord towards the Clayton area. It was too high for a helicopter. It's hard to guess, but I would say it was at least two thousand feet up, and it moved quickly"

The sighting remains unexplained to this day.

50- Clayton's Own Civil War-of Words

This story has been told to me by a few different people over the past five months. All telling of the story have slightly different endings, But isn't that what folklore is all about?

The story goes, that at the end of the civil war, many Southern troops made their way to the Clayton area to try and forge out a living. The area was also made up of many native whites that had Union connections. Many of these Southern men moved into town and pitched their tents in or near the grove while spending their days in the saloons and trying to find work. With bellies full of beer, these men reminisced about the old days and marched themselves through town chanting pro Southern slogans and causing general trouble with the locals.

Verbal outbursts flared up and often a few punches were thrown, but no real harm occurred. The Confederates were rounded up and dragged to the center of town and made to swear an oath to the stars and stripes. Most of these men were forced into reciting the oath then released. They staggered back to their tents and were not seen until the next afternoon when they would emerge from their slumber a lot worse for wear. Then by night fall, the activity started all over again with another march through town, more scuffles and more men made to swear on the flag. No weapons were ever used and no one spent more than a day in the town jail that now sits behind the Clayton Historical Society.

This is where the story takes a different turn depending on who you talk to. Some say the men were Southern sympathizers and others say Confederate soldiers. Others believe it was a group of rowdy miners who just liked to cause trouble. There was said to be a confrontation outside the place called the Eagle Club. Supposedly, a drunken Southerner got into a fight with a uniformed Northern officer who was mounted on his horse. The argument got heated and the officer took a swing at the Southerner who was on foot. The man staggered back and enraged, pulled his pistol and shot the officer out of his saddle and left him to die in the street. This story has not been verified and is now classed as part of the Clayton folklore.

51 – Canesa's Strange Room

With the book coming to an end, I want to add another layer to the activities that have been reported in the Clayton area. I am not sure if it falls under the title of a "portal" or just the presence of a paranormal entity.

There is a very small building, located between Skipolini's Pizza and the bocce ball courts. They make New York style subs that are by far my favorite in the area. The building is part of one of the older homes in the Clayton down town area. It is only about fifteen feet wide and about forty-five feet deep; it also offers a great outside dining area. At one end is a small serving area with a small office and refrigerator off to the left. This is the room that causes staff members to forget what they were coming to get. This has happened to all members of the staff and not just once in a while. Even a new employee named Shannon said she had forgotten what she was retrieving when entering the room. She was unaware that the phenomenon occurred for her coworkers when this story was relied to me. Connie, the manager, said the room has a heavy feeling, as if you are in water. The feeling is supported by the owner, John, who has experienced this feeling since moving into the building many years ago. He said that there is "High Energy that flows through the back portion of the building."

Another person came in while we were talking; I believe his name was Marco. Marco said he felt like it could be a portal or entrance to another dimension. Forgetting everything when you walk in a room and feeling weightless is very unnerving. I inspected the room, but I felt nothing at that time. I did notice that this was only half of what the original house that stood on this site. If the game room from Skipolini's Pizza was haunted, this could be the same spirit moving throughout the old house. I am told that the energy is much different than next door.

52- Not All Buildings Have Ghosts You Know

It has taken me over eight months to put together this collection of folklore, ghost stories, UFO accounts, Bigfoot encounters, Cryptozoology etc. and I want to let everyone that reads this book know, that the people of Clayton California are by far the nicest and easiest people I have ever worked with on any book I have produced. Everyone has opened up to me and many stopped what they were doing to give me a few minutes of their time to tell me their tales. I have made many new friends in this small community over the last eight months.

There were a few stops on my hunt for stories that had said there was no form of paranormal activity seen in their buildings or even in the skies around the area. To those people I say thank you for at least listening to me pitch my book.

Cup O' Jo Coffee shop states there is no ghosts or hauntings in the building, but I was then told that they once had to do a paranormal cleansing as a few customers were experiencing the spirit of a Native American on the property. Many of the newer structures claimed no activity.

53- Other Well Known Sites Not Included

Now you have come to the end of this book and you have read all the accounts I had the honor to work on in the past 8 months. Every story in this book has been researched by me and, with the exception of a few articles; all the stories have additional information supplied. This info comes from interviews with people in the area. There are a few stories that just found a dead end, this is due to no-one else knowing of the stories, people dying or just the same facts being passed around.

With the hours upon hours of news reports, library time and interviews I have managed to put together this updated collection of lore.

It is often asked of me where these locations are and to whom should one talk to gain access. Many of the people I have met did not what their name mentioned or they wanted an altered name to help protect their privacy. In some cases, the stories will not tell of an exact location. This is also for privacy reasons.

Even though I personally know of all the locations and have been inside most of the buildings mentioned, I promised not to reveal where the stories took place.

Even though most people have been receptive to my approach for an interview and their stories of the folklore, there are a few that did not want to be part of the book. To those people I say thanks for listening to my pitch. Unfortunately, their stories will fade into oblivion. To the others that opened up to me, I thank them for keeping local history and folklore relevant and alive.

54- Resources Used

THANK YOU TO THE FOLLOWING

http://www.theshadowlands.net

http://www.forgottenusa.com

http://www.hauntedplaces.org

www.mufon.com

www.ufocasebook.com

www.ufosightingsdaily.com

http://www.archives.gov/foia/ufos.html

http://www.nuforc.org

www.bfro.net

http://www.claytonclubsaloon.com

claytonhistorysociety.org

www.contracostatimes.com

Legends of Mount Diablo

Dorothy H. Huggins

Western Folklore Vol. 7, No. 2 (Apr., 1948)

www.fatemag.com

Louis DiMieri

Wing, Renee. Clayton Chronicles. April, 2015

San Francisco Academy of Sciences

Contra Costa Historical Society

Projects SIGN & GRUDGE

S.E. Schlosser

Bob Benjamin

Chabot Space and Science Center

KPIX-TV

Claycord News And Talk

Merriam – Webster dictionary

Jenny Hosel

Cindyriggs.com

Andrea Allison

http://hauntedhouses.com

Gary Bogue

Mysterious America

Dr. Shawn Robinson

http://www.crimezzz.net

Elisebeth Wetsch

City of Clayton Police Department.

SOTT.net

Contra Costa County Library System

Canesa's Brooklyn Heros

JoAnn Caspar

Richard Ellis

Ms. M

Martin Easton

Peter Matheson

Richard Taylor

Ms. E

Joaquin Murrieta Chapter No. 13 E Clampus Vitus

PLEASE SUPPORT THE BUSINSSES THAT HAVE HELPED SUPPORT ME & HELPED WRITE THIS BOOK.

City of Clayton Police Department

City of Clayton

The Clayton Club

Clayton Community Library

Clayton Historical Society, Museum and Library

Frontier Salon

The Royal Rooster

Ed's Mudville Grill

Cup O' Jo Coffee Shop

La Veranda Cafe Restaurant

Skipolini's Pizza

Moresi's Chop House

Canesa's Brooklyn Heros

Performance Trailer Services

Oakhurst Country Club

Contra Costa County Library System

Clayton Community Church

Claycord News And Talk

Contra Costa Times

Chabot Space and Science Center

Contra Costa Historical Society

San Francisco Academy of Sciences

Black Diamond Brewing Company

The Pioneer Newspaper